THE CASE OF THE CRAU   ..ISONERS DURING
THE LAND WAR IN CO. GALWAY, 1879–85

The case of the Craughwell prisoners during the Land War in Co. Galway, 1879–85

The law must take its course

Pat Finnegan

For Michael & Anne Fahy with kind regards

Pat Finnegan

FOUR COURTS PRESS

This book was set in 10.5 on 12.5 point Ehrhardt by
Mark Heslington, Scarborough, North Yorkshire for
FOUR COURTS PRESS
7 Malpas Street, Dublin 8, Ireland
www.fourcourtspress.ie
and in North America for
FOUR COURTS PRESS
c/o ISBS, 920 N.E. 58th Avenue, Suite 300, Portland, OR 97213.

A catalogue record for this title
is available from the British Library.

ISBN 978-1-84682-358-9 | hbk
ISBN 978-1-84682-359-6 | pbk

Printed in Great Britain
by Antony Rowe Ltd, Chippenham, Wilts.

Contents

Figures and tables

Abbreviations

AG	attorney general
CBS	crime branch special
CC	Catholic curate
CDB	Congested Districts Board
CI	county inspector
CRF	criminal record file
CS	crown solicitor
CSO	chief secretary's office
DI	district inspector
DM	divisional magistrate
Fr	Father (Roman Catholic priest)
GAA	Gaelic Athletic Association
HC	head constable
ILL	Irish Land League
INL	Irish National League
IRA	Irish Republican Army
IRB	Irish Republican Brotherhood
MP	member of parliament (UK)
NAI	National Archives of Ireland
NUIG	National University of Ireland, Galway
PAA	Prisoners Amnesty Association
PP	parish priest
QC	queen's counsel
Revd	Reverend
RIC	Royal Irish Constabulary
RM	resident magistrate
RP	registered papers
SI	sub inspector
SRM	special resident magistrate
TCD	Trinity College Dublin
TTA	Town Tenants Association
UIL	United Irish League

To the memory of
Patrick Finnegan and Michael Muldowney
and all those who have suffered from a miscarriage of justice

Preface and acknowledgments

During the Land War of 1879–82, south Galway was described as a dangerously disturbed area in which a large number of agrarian outrages occurred. Between May 1881 and June 1882, eight people were murdered, including a landlord (Walter Bourke of Rahasane House) and his soldier bodyguard, the land agent of Lord Clanrickarde and his servant, and three victims of land disputes. One of those killed was a young man called Peter Doherty from Carrigan near Craughwell. The killing took place after a dispute over land and the family was boycotted as a result. Threatening notices had been displayed and shots fired at the house. In November 1881, Peter Doherty was shot dead by a party of men. Two innocent men, Patrick Finnegan from Aggard and Constable Michael Muldowney, who had been on protection duty in Rahasane, were convicted of the killing and sentenced to death. Following the commutation of the death sentences, they spent twenty years in jail and became known as the 'Craughwell prisoners'.

My father, P.J. Finnegan, carried out preliminary searches of newspaper accounts of the trials and he also examined prison registers. My sister, Anne Ó'Máille, completed her MA thesis on the Land War in south Galway and she shared with me her extensive knowledge of that period. As a student, I visited the National Library and read some of the newspaper accounts of the trials. However, the task of writing the history of the Craughwell prisoners had to be postponed until retirement from a busy medical career. That my grandfather's history was still well known in the Craughwell area quickly became evident on my return to Galway in 1976. A number of hospital patients whom I encountered were aware of the story and the injustice of the murder convictions. Some individuals suggested names of those allegedly involved in the killing of Peter Doherty. Also around that time, the Craughwell parish magazine, *The Blazer*, edited by the late Revd Martin Coen, published a number of articles containing some details of the story.

My initial researches concentrated on newspaper archives in the Hardiman Library of the National University of Ireland, Galway, and the Galway County Library in Nuns Island. These searches revealed specific dates for the killing of Peter Doherty and the arrests and trials of the men charged with the murder. The next phase of the research, in the National Archives, concentrated on the voluminous registers and files of the chief secretary's papers. A wealth of detail was uncovered, including reports from investigating magistrates and police, the notes of the judge during one of Muldowney's trials, and the judge's reports to the lord lieutenant, Earl Spencer. Detailed information regarding the various informers included carefully kept records of payments, the clothing purchased for them and the arrangements made for their 'disposal' when they were no longer needed by the authorities. The prison records of Finnegan and Muldowney contained the numerous petitions that affirmed their innocence and pleaded for their pardon and release. Members of parliament, prominent citizens and local authorities in Galway and Leitrim also submitted petitions to no avail. The unfailing rejection of all petitions was accompanied by the statement that 'the law must take its course'.

Two local historians, Maura Lyons and Gerry Cloonan, played a very important role in the project. They generously shared with me their extensive knowledge of local history and guided my explorations of the scene of the killing and the surrounding area. An illustration of the Doherty homestead by Maura Lyons is reproduced with her kind permission. Gerry Cloonan supplied me with a copy of a letter written by Michael Clasby of Craughwell to my grandfather in Mountjoy Jail in 1900. He also shared verses composed shortly after the trials recounting the story of the killing of Peter Doherty and the sentences handed down. The late Andy Feeney, Killeeneen, provided helpful information and I was privileged to interview, shortly before he died, Denis Creaven of Greenhouse, who knew my grandfather over many years. I was delighted to meet Brendan Muldowney, the great grand-nephew of Michael Muldowney, who provided valuable information about the family.

Many institutions and libraries provided resources for the research. I am deeply grateful to the staff of the James Hardiman Library of NUIG and the Galway County Library for their unfailing professional help and kindness in guiding me through uncharted territory. Special thanks are due to Marie Boran and Kieran Hoare, and to Geraldine Curtin, who located the autobiography of James Berry. I was greatly assisted by the staff of the National Library of Ireland, the British Library and the National Archives of Ireland, especially by Bernadette Kelly and Aideen Ireland, and by Gregory O'Connor, who located the prison file of Michael Muldowney.

I am deeply grateful to Dr Fergus Campbell, Reader in History at Newcastle upon Tyne University. He was my inspirational advisor from the beginning of the project and his critical reading of the manuscript was an enormous help. I am also indebted to Professor James Donnelly, University of Wisconsin–Madison, who provided valuable critical advice during his periods of sabbatical leave in Galway. Dr John Cunningham and Dr Tony Varley and many other former colleagues and friends at NUIG provided helpful advice and encouragement. I gratefully acknowledge the grant towards publication of the book by the National University of Ireland, Galway.

I am grateful to Martin Fanning and Michael Potterton of Four Courts Press for their expert advice and commitment to the publication of this book.

My main debt is to my family. My wife Máire was a constant support and tolerated with great patience my many absences during the research and composition of the book. My children, Emer, Nuala and Niall, and my sister Anne Ó'Máille showed continuous interest in the project and also provided critical readings of the manuscript. My sister Alice, brother Paul and sister Mary were a constant support.

I would have been unable to complete the project without the enthusiastic participation of Marianne ten Cate and her critical scrutiny of the material. Her meticulous attention to proof reading and editing determined the final shape of the book.

Introduction

In early August 1884, Patrick Finnegan entered a railway carriage in Mullingar accompanied by a number of officers of the Royal Irish Constabulary. He had been convicted of murder at Sligo summer assizes and was *en route* to Galway Jail to be hanged three weeks later. As a result of a dispute over land, a young man called Peter Doherty had been shot dead in November 1881 in Carrigan near Craughwell, Co. Galway. Six local men were arrested in connection with the crime and, in Galway Jail, Finnegan would join Michael Muldowney, a constable in the RIC who had been convicted of the same crime two weeks earlier and was awaiting death by hanging on 12 August 1884.

When Finnegan boarded the train he was seated opposite two men who spoke with broad Yorkshire accents. The RIC guard introduced him to one of the men, James Berry, who, with his assistant, was travelling to Galway for the express purpose of hanging Finnegan and Muldowney.

How did the convicted men find themselves in Galway Jail under sentence of death? The answer lies in the dangerously disturbed nature of south Galway at that time. Between May 1881 and June 1882, eight people were murdered within a triangle joining Loughrea, Athenry and Ardrahan. The village of Craughwell is situated close to the centre of the triangle (fig. 1, p. 16).

The townlands of Carrigan East and Carrigan West, which formed part of the Rahasane estate, are near Rahasane turlough, 3.2km (two miles) from Craughwell. The Doherty family lived in Carrigan East, and one member, Peter Junior, was shot dead on the night of 2 November 1881. The killing arose from a dispute over a plot of land that to this day is known as the 'boycott' and the story of the killing and the fate of the accused men is still told in the locality.[1] The six local men accused of the murder of Peter Doherty became known as the Craughwell prisoners.

A complex interaction of political and social factors determined the circumstances leading to the troubled condition of this part of Co. Galway. The district, like others throughout the country, was affected by the profound changes that occurred before, during and after the Great Famine. Between 1841 and 1851, emigration and the increase in the death rate due to starvation and disease led to a major reduction of the population. The dramatic demographic changes are evident in the population trends in the Poor Law Unions of Loughrea and Gort between 1841 and 1861 (table 1, p. 17).

Over the period of twenty years, the population in the Loughrea Union decreased by 59 per cent and in Gort Union by 53 per cent, with the major

---

1 *The Blazer*, 11 (1982) (ed. Revd Martin Coen).

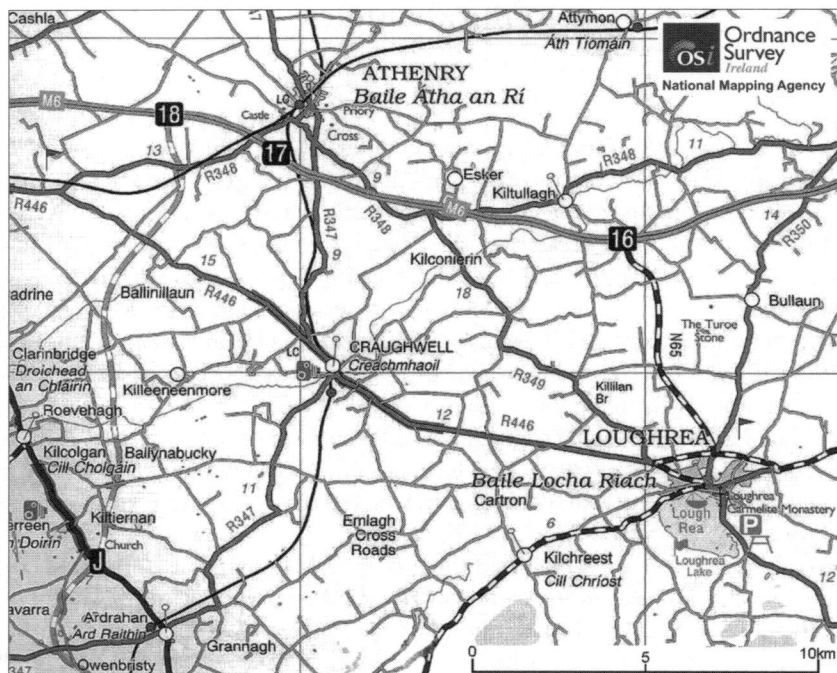

1 The murder triangle: Loughrea–Athenry–Ardrahan (source: *Official road atlas
Ireland, 2012–13* (Dublin & Belfast, 2011), Ordnance Survey Ireland permit 8815
© Ordnance Survey Ireland/Government of Ireland).

reduction occurring between 1841 and 1851. The continuing loss of people
between 1851 and 1861 indicates the impact of evictions and emigration. Typical
population changes in townlands within the Loughrea and Gort Unions are
shown in table 2 (p. 17).

The Encumbered Estates (Ireland) Act of 1849 was enacted in order to deal
with the bankruptcy of many Irish estates. Under the act, solvent members of
the aristocracy such as lords Clanrickarde, Clancarty, Ashtown and Dunsandle,
as well as a host of landed gentry, made extensive purchases.[2] Other purchasers
who were interested in the creation of large grazing farms to be run on a strictly
commercial basis came from England and Scotland. Between March and
December 1851, a total of 1,223 occupiers were cleared in Galway East Riding
and 3,570 in Galway West Riding.[3] The reduction in the amount of land devoted

2 Padraig G. Lane, 'The Encumbered Estates Court and Galway land ownership, 1849–58' in
Gerard Moran & Raymond Gillespie (eds), *Galway: history and society* (Dublin, 1996), pp
395–419.   3 Padraig G. Lane, 'The general impact of the Encumbered Estates Act of 1849 on
Counties Galway and Mayo', *Journal of Galway Archaelogical and Historical Society*, 33 (1972–3),
44–74.

Table 1 Population change in the Loughrea and Gort Poor Law Unions, 1841–61 (sources: Christine Kinealy, 'The response of the Poor Law to the Great Famine in Co. Galway', p. 390; P.G. Lane, 'The Encumbered Estates Court and Galway land ownership, 1849–58' in Gerard Moran and Raymond Gillespie (eds), *Galway: history and society* (Dublin, 1996), p. 412).

	1841	*1851*	*Change*	*1861*	*Change*	*Total change*
Loughrea	71,774	38,735	-46%	29,138	-25%	-59%
Gort	43,543	26,759	-39%	20,501	-23%	-53%

Table 2 Population change in south Galway townlands, 1841–51 (source: Sister Mary de Lourdes Fahy, *Kiltartan: many leaves, one root* (Kiltartan, 2004), p. 86).

	1841	*1851*	*Change*
Ardrahan	4,191	2,887	-31%
Kilchreest	1,579	954	-40%
Killeeneen	1,531	1,014	-34%
Killora	1,618	1,180	-27%
Kilogilleen	1,074	699	-35%

to labour-intensive tillage inevitably resulted in a loss of employment for labourers and a marked increase in emigration. The consolidation of holdings meant the creation of a distinct group known as graziers and the development of social and class conflicts with the small tillage farmers. The numbers of sheep and cattle on the land increased dramatically and, with rising prices for stock and low labour costs, the large farmers and graziers prospered. The small farmers throughout Galway participated in this commerce by the production of store cattle that were sold for fattening to eastern counties and Britain. Shopkeepers were also active in the acquisition of encumbered and evicted properties and they became deeply involved in the expanding cattle trade after the Famine.

Thomas Appleyard Joyce of Galway purchased the Rahasane estate in the first year of the Great Famine, 1846. At that time, there were a number of hovels in Carrigan West, close to the demesne wall. The wife of the new landlord expressed displeasure at the proximity of the unsightly dwellings and her husband ordered their levelling and the removal of the tenants to Carrigan East. Revd Thomas Cawley, a native of Craughwell, wrote *An Irish parish: its sunshine and shadows*, in which he referred to the removal of tenants from rich soil to a rocky townland nearby that he called 'Carraigeens'.[4] When Griffith's valuations were published in 1855, only one tenant, John Connolly, remained in Carrigan

4 Revd Thomas Cawley, *An Irish parish: its sunshine and shadows* (Boston, 1911), p. 31.

West, with a holding of sixty-four acres. There were thirty-six in Carrigan East and, of these, twenty-six had holdings of less than fifteen acres.[5] Peter Doherty Senior was included, with a holding of twelve acres. The Rahasane estate experienced financial difficulties and in 1870 Walter Bourke, a native of Mayo, acquired the estate. He proved to be a harsh landlord who created many enemies among his tenants. He was assassinated along with his soldier bodyguard in June 1882 (see below, pp 24–7).

The period of relative prosperity across much of Ireland between 1863 and 1876 was also experienced in the Craughwell area. There was a succession of good harvests and a significant improvement in the prices for stock and agricultural produce. Social conditions also improved, with a marked increase in literacy rates. The politicization of local communities was greatly facilitated by the proliferation of national and local newspapers. The political control exerted by landlords on parliamentary elections began to wane and nationalists increasingly challenged their dominance on the boards of Poor Law Unions. However, the period of prosperity ended with a succession of bad harvests in the late 1870s, and the agricultural crisis of 1879–80 generated fears of another major famine. The intervention of charitable organizations and private sources ensured that a major catastrophe was averted. In contrast, there was strong criticism of the tardy and limited response of the government. The newly formed Land League distributed £60,000 that had been collected in America and took the opportunity to establish Land League branches throughout the country. In November 1879, Lord Clanrickarde rejected a plea from tenants on his Craughwell estate for a reduction in rent and threatened the eviction of every tenant failing to pay in full.[6] In response to this threat, a branch of the Land League was formed and the local communities quickly became involved in the ferment of political activity that evolved between 1879 and 1882.

There was a tradition of agrarian secret societies in the area from the early eighteenth century, including the Right Boys and the Whiteboys. The most famous local individual was Anthony Daly, who was regarded as the leader of the Whiteboys. Following attacks on Roxborough House, Raford House and St Clerans in 1820, he was arrested, convicted and executed at Seefin between Craughwell and Loughrea.[7] The poet Antoine Raifterí, who was very familiar with south Galway at that period, commemorated Daly in his poem *Antoine Ó Dálaigh*, and also referred to Whiteboy activity in poems entitled *Na buachailli bána*.[8] The resurgence of these societies during the Land War of 1879–82 had a very important bearing on local militant behaviour. In conjunction with the Fenian movement, their activities were largely responsible for the reputation of south Galway as a 'disturbed' area. It is probable that armed groups of Fenian

5 Maura Lyons, unpublished history of Rahasane House. 6 *Western News*, 29 Nov. 1879.
7 David Ryan, 'The trial and execution of Anthony Daly' in *Loughrea history project*, i, p. 99.
8 Antoine Raifteri (1784–1835), born in Killeadan, Co. Mayo, buried in Killeeneen, Co. Galway.

members amalgamated with local agrarian societies and that they formed units to carry out the more serious acts of violence. The government became alarmed because of the dramatic increase in what was known as agrarian outrages, and the chief secretary, William Edward Forster, introduced the Protection of Person and Property (Ireland) Act that became law in March 1881.[9] Popularly known as the Coercion Act, it resulted in the arrest and internment without trial of a considerable number of suspects from the Loughrea and Athenry police districts. One hundred and eleven men (see below, appendix 1) were arrested in the Loughrea and Athenry police districts, representing 11 per cent of the national total of arrests made. The fact that eight agrarian killings as well as many other agrarian crimes occurred in the area was the stimulus for the arrests and the identification of Loughrea as a 'den of infamy'. The killings were all deemed to be agrarian crimes.

Although many arrests were made under the Protection of Person and Property (Ireland) Act of 1881 and the Prevention of Crime (Ireland) Act of 1882, only twelve individuals were charged with the killings. Two were acquitted and pleas of *nolle prosequi* were entered in eight cases. The only convictions achieved by the crown in relation to the eight killings were in the case of Peter Doherty of Carrigan, in which two innocent men, Michael Muldowney and Patrick Finnegan, were convicted and sentenced to death in 1884. A major focus of the present book is the circumstances of that killing, the arrest of the six accused men and the trials of Muldowney and Finnegan. The book argues that their convictions were flagrant miscarriages of justice based on deeply flawed evidence and the perjured testimony of two informers of disreputable character. The part played by informers was crucial to the outcome of the trials and a detailed account outlines the protection accorded them, the payments made to them and their eventual 'disposal' by the Dublin Castle authorities. Judicial practices are examined, including the authority of the attorney general to change the venue of trials, and the prevalent practice of jury packing, both of which had an important influence on the verdicts reached in the trials.

Following the convictions of Muldowney and Finnegan, several petitions were sent to Dublin Castle pleading for the commutation of their death sentences. The lord lieutenant, Lord Spencer, held consultations with Judge Murphy (fig. 6, p. 49), who had presided at the trials, and the lord chancellor before deciding to reprieve the prisoners and sentence them to penal servitude for life. The experiences of the prisoners in Mountjoy and Maryborough jails are revealed from the prison files and these files also contain the multiple petitions that affirmed their innocence and pleaded for their pardon and release. The subtitle of this book refers to the invariable response of successive lords lieutenant of Ireland to their pleas: 'the law must take its course'. Finally, the book deals with the Craughwell prisoners' experiences after their release from prison.

9 Protection of Person and Property (Ireland) Act, 44 & 45 Vict. 1881.

1 Agrarian incidents in south Galway

At the end of May 1880, an event occurred in Craughwell that was to cast a long shadow over the coming years. Thomas Cunniffe relinquished a holding of land in Carrigan that he had rented from Walter Bourke of Rahasane House. Peter Doherty Senior and his cousin John Doherty agreed to rent the land. Protests were reported immediately, the windows of the Dohertys' houses were broken, shots were fired and afterwards police patrols were provided for their protection.[1] Placards denouncing land grabbers were posted throughout the Craughwell area and threatening letters were sent to local landlords in relation to proposed evictions.

Land meetings attended by large crowds were held and at Riverville on 19 September the focus was on the eviction of Martin Bermingham on the Dunsandle estate. A man called Murty Hynes took the holding but he quickly yielded to public pressure and gave up the land. However, a subsequent tenant, Peter Dempsey was to forfeit his life in May 1881. Local bands and large numbers of men carrying sticks and swords who marched in military order attended other meetings at Ballymana and Craughwell.

An increase in the number of evictions in the latter part of 1880 inevitably inflamed passions in the countryside and it is not surprising that agrarian crimes increased in frequency. John W. Lambert of Aggard House, the owner of an estate of 3,440 acres, was an early target when a large grave was dug in front of his house and a document was found close by, stating 'that if he did not cease persecuting his tenants he would shortly be consigned to the grave'.[2] Lambert, in evidence to the Special (Times–Parnell) Commission,[3] said that he was boycotted for three years, tenants surrendered some 600 acres, walls were knocked, workmen left his employment and the houses of two herds were burned down. He was given police protection and 'Emergency men were sent from Liverpool to work for him'.[4] He complained that they knew nothing about the work and they were more of a nuisance. His brother, Walter P. Lambert of Castle Ellen, Athenry, was also boycotted and his domestic staff and herdsmen were warned to leave his employment.[5] Other episodes included armed attacks on Captain Smyth of Masonbrook, Loughrea,[6] and a bailiff collecting rent.[7] For

---

1 *Western News*, 19 June 1880.   2 *Irish Times*, 13 Oct. 1880.   3 The Special (Times-Parnell) Commission was established by the Tory government in 1888 to investigate allegations in the *Times* that Parnell and other leaders of the Land League had been involved in crime during the Land War.   4 NLI Parnell Special Commission, i, pp 483–4.   5 *Irish Times*, 22 Nov. 1880. 6 *Irish Times*, 30 Aug. 1880.   7 *Irish Times*, 4 Oct. 1880.

the second time in 1880, Peter Blake of Hollypark received a letter threatening him with instant death if he evicted a poor woman from his property. The letter was signed 'Rory of the Hills'.[8]

James Morrissey from Carrigan was involved in an attempt to bring arms from Barna to Craughwell in June 1880. The attempt failed when the shipment was intercepted by the RIC at Oranmore. However, the local availability of arms was enhanced with the larceny of fifteen rifles in transit from Limerick to Loughrea.[9] They were taken from a store at Craughwell railway station and it was believed by the police that Edward Barrett of Craughwell was the organizer of the raid.[10] The ready availability of arms and the appearance at many meetings of contingents marching in military order indicate the developing influence of the Fenian movement within the Land League organization.

8 *Irish Times*, 12 Dec. 1880. 9 *Irish Times*, 18 Nov. 1880. 10 NAI CSO RP 1883/153.

2 The murder triangle, 1881–2

INTRODUCTION

Between May 1881 and June 1882, eight people were murdered in a triangle bounded by Loughrea, Athenry and Ardrahan, Co. Galway. The victims included a landlord and his guard, the agent of Lord Clanrickarde and his driver, a policeman and three tenants who had transgressed the Land League prohibition on taking lands deemed to belong to evicted tenants. The killings illustrate the whole spectrum of crimes of that period that were considered to be agrarian in nature. Although many of the acts of violence during the Land War were carried out in winter under the cover of darkness, these killings, with one exception, occurred in summer and in daylight hours. This may well reflect a sense of impunity from detection felt by the perpetrators and the supportive collusion of the local communities. It is possible that the disciplined units of the Irish Republican Brotherhood could enforce this wall of silence in the same way that the Irish Republican Army achieved the same objective in a later era.

After each killing there were widespread consequences, initially associated with the police and magisterial investigations and the preliminary court hearings. A large number of suspects were arrested in each location and many of the detentions were obtained under the terms of the Protection of Person and Property (Ireland) Act of 1881 and were frequently based on dubious circumstantial evidence. The influx of large numbers of police and military contributed to the already heightened tensions in the area and the local communities were also faced with the tax levied for the maintenance of the additional security forces. Finally, the ratepayers of the affected districts were financially penalized by the compensation payments to the families of the victims.

THE KILLING OF JAMES CONNORS, 13 MAY 1881

The first murder of the year occurred on 13 May when James Connors, Killariff, Kiltulla, was shot at Forge Hill, Bookeen. Connors was a small farmer with a holding of fourteen acres under Lord Dunsandle. He had become a bog ranger or gamekeeper on the estate, a job previously held by James Keogh, who had been ordered to resign the position by the Kiltulla Land League. When Connors took the job he was boycotted, food had to be supplied to the family by the police and he was abused as a land grabber.[1] The post mortem conducted by Dr

---

1 NLI Parnell Special Commission, i, p. 473.

Leonard, Athenry, revealed that Connors' death was caused by a single bullet that passed through the left lung.[2]

On 4 June three men were arrested, Timothy Dolan, secretary of the Kiltulla Land League, Patrick Keogh, also a member of the Land League and son of the previous bog ranger, and another member of the Land League, Edward Fahey. A fourth, John Ryan, was arrested on 16 June. At the magisterial inquiry held in Loughrea Courthouse, Sub Inspector Dominick Barry, who was in charge of the investigation, stated that because of the reluctance of the people to cooperate, he was unable to produce any material evidence. The prisoners' solicitor demanded their release and the magistrates consented. However, as they left Loughrea Courthouse they were arrested under the Protection of Person and Property (Ireland) Act of 1881 on the grounds that they were suspected of murder. They remained in jail until August 1882, when there was a general release of arrested 'suspects'. Eventually, Patrick Keogh and John Ryan were brought to trial. After several adjournments, the trial took place at the summer assizes in Sligo (fig. 5, p. 48) in 1883 before Judge James Murphy (fig. 6, p. 49). The court was told of conflicting evidence given by Mrs Julia Connors on different occasions. Judge Murphy charged in favour of Keogh's acquittal and the crown then entered a plea of *nolle prosequi* in relation to John Ryan.[3]

THE KILLING OF PETER DEMPSEY, 29 MAY 1881

The farm at Riverville, which had been vacated by Murty Hynes, lay vacant until April 1881 when it was taken by a man called Peter Dempsey. Dempsey was boycotted and on 29 May, on his way to Mass in Kilconieron Church with two of his children, he was shot dead at Hollypark.[4] Martin Bermingham, the evicted tenant, was arrested and confined in Galway Jail until August 1882. He was never brought to trial for the killing. Local knowledge suggests that the killing of Dempsey was carried out by members of a Craughwell secret society and that the Joyce brothers, Thomas and Dominick of Ballywinna, Craughwell, were selected by lot to shoot Dempsey.

THE KILLING OF CONSTABLE JAMES LINTON, 24 JULY 1881

Constable Linton, a native of Co. Down, aged forty-two years, had been stationed in Loughrea for twenty years and had gained a reputation for discharging his duties with great diligence, particularly regarding breaches of the licensing laws.

2 *Irish Times*, 16 May 1881.   3 *Tuam News*, 4 Aug. 1883.   4 *Irish Times*, 31 May 1881.

At 10pm on Sunday 24 July, while returning to barracks for roll call, Linton was fired at and mortally wounded outside the Protestant Church in Church Street. Two men were arrested in February 1883, a publican named Michael Dilleen and a leading IRB member, John McCarthy. The trial of Dilleen took place in December 1883 at the winter assizes in Sligo. Although one witness claimed that Linton had 'cried out "Dilleen shot me"', the rest of the evidence was tenuous and conflicting and the crown entered a plea of *nolle prosequi*.[5]

THE KILLING OF PETER DOHERTY AT CARRIGAN, 2 NOVEMBER 1881

On the night of 2 November 1881, a young man called Peter Doherty was shot dead at Carrigan, close to Rahasane House and a few kilometres from Craughwell (see below, chs 3, 4, 5).

THE KILLING OF WALTER BOURKE AND
CORPORAL WALLACE, 8 JUNE 1882

Although there were to be no killings in the area for seven months and no mass public meetings, the district was thrown into turmoil again with four more killings during June 1882. There was continuing agrarian unrest and threatening notices were regularly posted for employees of John Lambert, Walter Bourke and Burton Persse. Bourke of Rahasane House and his soldier bodyguard, Corporal Robert Wallace, were shot dead on 8 June. In 1870, Bourke had purchased almost 2,000 acres at Rahasane and also inherited substantial landholdings from his older brother near Claremorris, Co. Mayo. Relationships with his tenants on both estates were difficult and he was widely regarded as a harsh landlord and a man of exceptional determination with a history of frequent evictions. When bailiffs could not be induced to serve ejectments, he served them himself and a famous sketch by Aloysius O'Kelly illustrates one such episode near Claremorris (fig. 2, p. 25).[6]

On another occasion, in Barnacarroll, Claremorris, Bourke insisted on bringing his rifle into the church and refused to leave when requested to do so by the priest. He considered that the rifle was essential for his protection because his life had been threatened on several occasions in both Mayo and Galway.

On 8 June, Walter Bourke attended the Gort Petty Sessions to obtain orders to evict his tenants in Carrigan. He was returning to Rahasane House when he and his guard, Corporal Robert Wallace of the Royal Dragoon Guards, were ambushed at Castletaylor and shot dead.[7] Bourke was armed with an eighteen-

5 *Tuam News*, 28 Dec. 1883.   6 *Illustrated London News*, 14 May 1881.   7 *Western News*, 10

2 'The Irish Land League agitation: Mr Walter Burke [*sic*] serving writs on his tenants. From a sketch by our special artist', *Illustrated London News*, 14 May 1881.

chamber Winchester rifle and Wallace had a carbine. The assailants took possession of the guns belonging to Bourke and Wallace and escaped through the Castletaylor fields in the direction of Craughwell. On the day following the shooting, great activity was reported in Galway, where conveyances of all descriptions were commissioned to carry thirty men of the 88th Connaught Rangers and ninety soldiers of the 84th York and Lancaster Regiment. These soldiers joined police and military from Loughrea, Gort and Athenry, giving a combined force of approximately three hundred. They searched 'every ditch, dike and wall for miles around'; three old guns were found but none were serviceable. Five sets of footprints near Castletaylor pointed in the direction of Craughwell.[8]

The inquest was held at Rahasane House[9] and Mr Shawe-Taylor, the landlord of Castletaylor, gave evidence that between 2pm and 3pm he was tending stock on his farm and afterwards walked towards the crossroads. As he approached, he heard five or six shots in succession. He saw five or six men, all armed and wearing frieze coats. He noticed that one of the men carried two guns. He said that he was unable to identify any of the men. 'The nearest man presented a gun at him for about half a minute, and then he took down the gun and walked on'.

June 1882. 8 *Galway Express*, 10 June 1882. 9 *Irish Times*, 10 June 1882.

At first, Shawe-Taylor thought the men were poachers, until he found Wallace lying in a pool of blood and Bourke lying against the wheel of the trap. Captain Amyatt Burney, 1st Royal Engineers, said that Bourke had three soldiers for protection purposes and normally two accompanied him. However, at the end of May he had indicated that he would prefer to have only one soldier guarding him. Mr Shawe-Taylor met the shooting party and there is a local belief that he recognized three of the shooting party – Brian Grealish, Brian Melvin from Killeeneen and Larry Deely of Gurraun – but did not inform the police.

Dr P.R. Dalton, Oranmore, performed the post mortem examination on Bourke and found five superficial gunshot wounds on the back of the neck. On the head there were seven wounds, two of which penetrated the brain and in his opinion death was instantaneous. Dr Charles Blake Lewis of the Army Medical Department carried out the examination on Robert Wallace. He found seven wounds, four entrance wounds and three exit wounds; they were all penetrating bullet wounds. The bullet that caused death left a penetrating wound above the right ear causing laceration of the brain.[10] Because of the nature of the wounds the assailants must have used both shotguns and rifles in the attack.

Walter Bourke was buried on 13 June in the family vault at Barnacarroll, Co. Mayo and Corporal Wallace was interred with full military honours at the military cemetery, Arbor Hill, Dublin.[11] In a letter to Prime Minister Gladstone soon after the shooting, Lord Spencer referred to Bourke as

> a very unpopular landlord, a proud and very harsh one, he had long been in great danger, indeed I saw a letter he wrote to the National Boards of Education in 1881 in which he stated he considered his life in such danger that he nominated his brother to succeed him as manager of the school.

Spencer further commented that

> there can be no doubt whatever of the existence of these secret societies in many parts of the country. It is essential to get at their organization and one can only effectually do this by undermining them and getting secret information which will lead up to conviction. We have offered rewards by thousands with no result.[12]

The following proclamation was published on 9 June in the *Dublin Gazette*:

> His Excellency, for the better apprehending and bringing to justice the perpetrators of these murders, is pleased hereby to offer a reward of

10 *Irish Times*, 10 June 1882.   11 *Galway Vindicator*, 14 June 1882.   12 BL Spencer papers, 76854, Spencer to Gladstone, 11 June 1882.

£2,000 and a further £1,000 for private information leading to conviction. A free pardon and the special protection of the crown in any part of Her Majesty's Dominions to anyone concerned in or privy to the murders other than those who actually committed it.

Even though a large number of arrests were made under the Prevention of Crime (Ireland) Act in July 1882, none of those arrested were charged with the Bourke killing.

There are a number of police claims that tradesmen from Dublin working at Tullira Castle and Tyrone House formed a branch of the Invincibles,[13] and P.J.P. Tynan attributed the 'suppression' of Bourke to the actions of the Invincibles.[14] However, local knowledge suggests that in addition to Grealish, Melvin and Deely, others alleged to have been involved were Martin and Michael Connolly of Ballymana and Bill Greene of Rathcosgrove. Three arrests were made near the scene of the killing, but Resident Magistrate David B. Franks discharged the men because of lack of evidence.[15] Furthermore, in a witness statement, Martin Newell claimed that the killing was organized locally and that his father John, who was Fenian Centre for the Barony of Dunkellin, knew about the plan for the shooting of Bourke.[16]

THE KILLING OF JOHN H. BLAKE AND THADY RUANE, 29 JUNE 1882

The two final killings took place on 29 June 1882, when, on the outskirts of Loughrea, John Henry Blake and his servant Thady Ruane were shot dead and Blake's wife was wounded. Blake was related to the Dalys of Raford and he moved from the family home in Furbo, Co. Galway, to become agent to his nephew. He lived at Rathville House, Kiltulla, and was appointed agent to Lord Clanrickarde in 1860. He was regarded as an unsympathetic individual, who, in carrying out the harsh instructions of Clanrickarde, incurred the enmity of tenants. However, there is evidence that he did try to ameliorate the intransigent attitudes of Clanrickarde, informing him of the more lenient behaviour of other landlords in the area. He had apparently submitted a letter of resignation from the post of agent in January 1882,[17] but he was clearly still working for Clanrickarde at the time of the killing because he was involved in the eviction of ten families in Pigott's Lane, Loughrea, in the same week.[18]

Blake, with his wife and driver, left Rathville House at 11am in order to travel

13 PRO CO 904/12, Precis of information and reports on secret societies, May 1910. 14 P.J.P. Tynan, *The Irish National Invincibles and their times* (London, 1894), p. 487. 15 *Irish Times*, 10 June 1882. 16 Military Archives, Bureau of Military History, WS 1,562, Martin Newell witness statement. 17 Catherine Kelly Desmond, 'John Henry Blake: villain or victim' in Kieran Jordan (ed.), *Kiltullagh/Killimordaly* (Midleton, 2000). 18 *Tuam News*, 30 June 1882.

to Loughrea to attend Mass on the day of a church holiday. Within a mile of the town, a shot was fired from behind a wall that struck Blake, knocking him from the car. Ruane tried to escape but was also hit and died instantly. Blake's wife, Henrietta Frances, a daughter of Dr Francis Lynch, Mount Pleasant, Loughrea, received a gunshot wound to the thigh. The bolting horse was stopped some distance down the road to Loughrea. Examination of the scene revealed that stones had been removed from the wall to make loopholes for the guns.[19] Drs O'Donohue, Leonard and Burke conducted the post mortem examinations and the inquest was held at Clanrickarde's agency office in Loughrea. The examinations revealed that a bullet had entered Blake's skull from behind and was responsible for his instant death.[20] A bullet in the head also caused the death of Thady Ruane, who was survived by his widow, six sons and five daughters.

Twenty-one people were arrested on 4 July in Loughrea under the Protection of Person and Property (Ireland) Act of 1881, suspected of involvement in the killing of Blake and Ruane. All the arrests were on charges of being accessories to murder or of conspiracy to murder. The suspects were released after six weeks and no one was prosecuted for the killings. The local opinion at the time was that members of an agrarian secret society and IRB members based in Rathruddy, on the outskirts of Loughrea, were responsible for the killings.

COMMUNITIES UNDER SIEGE

The murders committed between May 1881 and June 1882 had profound effects on the local communities. The events led to a marked increase in the numbers of police and military allocated to the area and an intensification of surveillance. The arbitrary powers of arrest under the Protection of Person and Property (Ireland) Act suggested that rank and file members of the Land League were at risk of arrest even though they had no connection with the IRB or other illegal societies. These fears were felt most acutely in the immediate locality of the killings and probably most of all in Loughrea. Following the killing of Constable Linton, Peter Sweeney, writing to his brother John in Galway Jail, captured the mood of anxiety engendered on the night of the killing when 'the police patrolled with heavy step and grim resolve and the work of ransacking went on with unabated zeal', inducing 'a terror that almost divested us of our thinking powers'. It was as if 'an invading army with the powers of plunder that marked the march of Cromwell came to us and encamped beside the lake'.[21] The sense of being under siege became even more oppressive after numerous arrests in January and February 1882 and also after the killing of Blake and Ruane at the end of June.

19 *Freeman's Journal*, 30 June 1882.   20 *Freeman's Journal*, 1 July 1882.   21 Private collection of the present author.

COMPENSATION HEARINGS

Under the provisions of the Prevention of Crime (Ireland) Act of 1882, compensation became payable to victims of crimes if they were proved to be agrarian in nature or the result of the actions of an unlawful society. In addition, the costs of the extra police and military deployments were levied on the localities in which the killings took place. The compensation hearings in relation to seven of the eight killings were held in Galway Record Court before Queen's Counsel Mr J. Alexander Byrne in November 1882.[22]

The first claim was that of Julia Connors, a mother of five children and widow of James Connors, Killariff. She received a sum of £800.[23] A similar sum was awarded to Mary Dempsey, widow of Peter Dempsey. There is no record of compensation to the brother of Constable Linton. Mrs Fanny Wallace claimed compensation for the death of her husband, Corporal Robert Wallace, and was awarded £300. The claims for compensation for the killing of Walter Bourke were heard in Claremorris Courthouse in November 1882. His brother and heir, Isidore Bourke, who was in surgical practice in London earning £1,500 per annum, claimed that he suffered severe financial loss because of frequent visits to Ireland since the death of his brother. He claimed compensation of £20,000.[24] The award made was £1,500, to be paid in three instalments.[25] An award of £3,000 was made to John Henry Blake's widow in relation to the death of her husband and £1,200 in compensation for her own injuries sustained in the shooting. The family of Blake's driver, Thady Ruane, was awarded the sum of £400. This could hardly be considered generous compensation for a widow and eleven children. The compensation hearing in relation to the death of Peter Doherty Junior will be dealt with in ch. 6.

LIABILITY IN RELATION TO COSTS OF POLICING AND COMPENSATION PAYMENTS

Because of the large number of killings in the area, the costs of the extra police and military constituted a severe additional burden, and the baronies of Loughrea and Athenry became liable for the enormous sum of £11,000. The awards are also of interest because of the marked disparity between the sums paid to the families of the gentry and the amounts given to their employees and to the families of the three farmer victims.[26] The authorities believed that the additional financial burden had a significant effect on the reduction of crime in the disturbed districts, especially when it was combined with intensive patrolling and saturation of the area with great numbers of police and military. However,

22 *Galway Vindicator*, 2 Dec. 1882.   23 HC 1884 (80), lxiii, 529.   24 *Galway Express*, 2 Dec. 1882.   25 HC 1884 (80), lxiii, 529.   26 Ibid.

there is no doubt also that from the community's viewpoint it generated considerable enmity towards the authorities and this may explain the exclusion of this
provision when the Prevention of Crime (Ireland) Act of 1882 was renewed in
1887.

3 The killing of Peter Doherty, 2 November 1881

INTRODUCTION

Intensive police investigations had continued following the killing of Peter Doherty in November 1881 and, on 26 January 1883, six men were arrested and charged with the killing. Four of those accused of the killing, Michael Connolly, Patrick Finnegan, Michael Fogarty and Thomas Joyce, had already been interned on suspicion of murder under the Protection of Person and Property (Ireland) Act of 1881 and released from jail in August 1882. Finnegan, Connolly and Fogarty were also jailed after an Irish National League meeting in Ballymana in December 1882 and had only one week's freedom before their return to Galway Jail. Following the arrests, there was a long period of magisterial investigation and eventually Michael Muldowney and Patrick Finnegan were brought to trial and convicted of the murder.

THE NIGHT OF THE KILLING

Peter Doherty Junior was shot dead at his home in Carrigan near Craughwell on the night of 2 November 1881 (fig. 3, p. 32). The Doherty family, Peter Senior and his wife Margaret, their only son Peter and two daughters, Mary Anne and Kate, lived on a farm of twelve acres in Carrigan East. Earlier that evening, Peter Junior had visited his cousin, John Doherty, who lived nearby in the direction of Rahasane House. Peter returned home at 8pm and the family ate supper together. After the meal, they were surprised to hear a horse moving about in the yard, because their horse had been fed and secured in the stable by Peter Senior an hour previously. Peter Junior and Kate went outside and Peter led the horse back to the stable. Kate returned to the house before him and immediately heard two gunshots in rapid succession. Kate and Mary Anne went to the front door and had a lucky escape when two bullets were fired through the doorway. They found Peter lying on his back outside the door. He said 'I am shot' and uttered a few words of prayer. With the help of Peter Senior, they carried him into the kitchen, at which stage they were certain he was dead.

ANTECEDENTS TO THE KILLING

RM Franks of Gort carried out the initial investigations and in his report to Dublin Castle he outlined the sequence of events that culminated in the death of

3 Painting of the Doherty house, by Maura Lyons.

Peter Doherty.[1] At the end of May 1880, Thomas Cunniffe had relinquished the twenty-acre holding of land in Carrigan (fig. 4, p. 41), which he had rented from Walter Bourke of Rahasane House. In a letter to the *Freeman's Journal* on 5 July, Cunniffe stated 'I have never asked for a reduction of rent of that land but have wished for the past two years to surrender it and to keep the rest of my holding'.[2] Three days after the shooting of Peter Doherty, Walter Bourke wrote to the *Freeman's Journal* confirming Cunniffe's account and enclosing a copy of Cunniffe's letter.[3] The Morrissey family of Carrigan applied for the land but were refused by Bourke. Peter Doherty Senior and his cousin John were granted the land instead. Peter Doherty Junior was requested to attend a meeting of the local Land League in Roveagh, Clarinbridge, where Patrick and James Morrissey appeared as witnesses.[4] The meeting condemned the acquisition of the land by the Dohertys and ordered them to vacate the property, but they refused to do so. A boycott was declared and various acts of intimidation followed. Within a month, shots were fired through the Doherty's windows and the mane and tail of their horse were cut. Some of their fences and about thirty yards of a stone wall were broken down. Police patrols were provided for their protection and placards posted in the vicinity were phrased in typical polemical style:

1 NAI CSO RP1881/38563 in 1881/41874. 2 *Freeman's Journal*, 5 July 1880. 3 *Freeman's Journal*, 7 Nov. 1881. 4 NAI ILL and INL documents, carton 10.

Regardless of warnings, two wretches are to be found in our midst who have taken land contrary to the rules of the Land League. Let those soulless wretches be excluded from society as some unclean things! Let no tenants be found in the locality to assist or work for them. Tenant farmers of Craughwell and surrounding districts be up and doing – Down with all land grabbers.[5]

During the winter of 1880, the Land League held a meeting in the field in front of Doherty's house and one of the speakers said 'they would make the Dohertys tremble like bulrushes in a stream'.[6] Peter Doherty Senior believed that James Regan, the steward at Rahasane House, was responsible for organizing the boycott and Regan was also suspected of posting threatening notices. On one occasion, Regan advised him to 'throw the land there to the devil', advice that he subsequently wished he had taken.[7] The Morrisseys engaged in regular abuse of the Dohertys and one of them warned Peter Junior that they would have a watch on him night and day.[8] Another serious incident occurred in March 1881, when several cattle were poisoned.[9] Regular police patrols were commenced to protect the Dohertys, but the intimidation and posting of notices continued. During October, Peter Doherty Junior brought Walter Bourke's cattle to the fair in Loughrea. A crowd gathered around him with a menacing attitude and called him names. He became alarmed and took refuge in the rent office of Lord Clanrickarde until he found an opportunity to leave safely.[10]

On Sunday 30 October, a notice was placed in Craughwell chapel advertising a cant or auction in the locality on 2 November. Peter Doherty was identified as the auctioneer and several articles that the Dohertys were known to possess, such as a sewing machine, were listed for auction. It was also known in the locality that there would be no protection patrols at Doherty's house on 2 November because a number of the local police and a large contingent from outside the area would be on duty protecting 'Emergency Men' working at Aggard House (fig. 4, p. 41).

AFTERMATH OF THE KILLING

Immediately after the shooting, Kate Doherty went to report the occurrence[11] to Constable James Laing in Craughwell Barracks. Constable Owen Judge was instructed to visit Carrigan to investigate. In view of the part they played in the boycott, it is not surprising that suspicion fell on the Morrisseys and the first person arrested was James Morrissey. A family member later stated that James was always attending meetings and that he was an officer in a secret society.[12]

5 *Irish Times*, 10 July 1880. 6 *Sligo Champion*, 15 Mar. 1884. 7 *Sligo Champion*, 19 July 1884. 8 *Sligo Champion*, 15 Mar. 1884. 9 NLI Parnell Special Commission, i, p. 512. Evidence of SI Alan Bell. 10 NAI ILL and INL documents, carton 10. 11 There is a local belief that she met Finnegan, who was returning from Craughwell, but did not recognize him. 12 Letter of

Constable Michael Muldowney, who was on protection duty at Rahasane House, joined Constable Judge and they arrested Thomas Cunniffe, the previous tenant of the disputed property. The following morning, SI Alan Bell, who was to play a key role in the investigations, visited Carrigan and was shown walls that were damaged near the house and also in the direction of John Doherty's. On the same morning James Morrissey's brother Patrick, and John Newell, the Fenian Head Centre for the barony of Dunkellin, were arrested.

RM Franks was concerned about the safety of the Dohertys and he instructed SI Bell to provide two policemen in Peter Doherty's house and constant patrols around John Doherty's. Franks also advised that 'a hut with an adequate force of police should be placed at Carrigan as the only probable remedy for controlling the frequent defiances of law and order'.[13] The iron hut was duly erected in Carrigan, on land belonging to the Morrisseys.

The local community in Carrigan was deeply shocked by the murder of Peter Doherty and it was believed that the Roveagh Land League members were dismayed because they expected that only warning shots were intended. Fr Skerret CC of Roveagh made a forthright statement condemning the killing.[14]

An early reaction in the chief secretary's residence is noted in Florence Arnold-Forster's journal entry for 6 November. A visitor, a cousin of Christopher Redington of Clarinbridge, told her that Redington 'is very unhappy about the disposition of the people round him'; he is 'very much depressed and despairs of getting his rents'. The murder of Peter Doherty was in his neighbourhood; 'it is believed to have been a judicial assassination, planned and executed by a secret society which had sentenced the man to death'. She concluded with the comment that 'as usual, no evidence is forthcoming and if there *were*, no jury would convict upon it'.[15]

THE INQUEST AND INITIAL COURT HEARINGS

The inquest into the death was held before District Coroner Mr E.K. Lynch, RM Byrne, Loughrea, and RM Franks, Gort. County Inspector Byrne, SI Dominick Barry, Loughrea, and SI Alan Bell, Athenry, represented the police. Dr P.R. Dalton, Oranmore, and Dr Leonard, Athenry, performed the post mortem examination and they reported that there were three bullet wounds on the body, a superficial wound over the left ear and entry and exit wounds of the bullet that caused death. This bullet entered at the left shoulder, passed through the left lung, spinal cord and right lung and made its exit behind the right shoulder. The jury returned an open verdict, that 'Peter Doherty was murdered by some person or persons unknown'.[16]

John (Soldier) Morrissey, courtesy of Maura Lyons. **13** NAI CSO RP 1881/38563 in 1881/41874. **14** *Galway Vindicator*, 9 Nov. 1881; *Galway Express*, 12 Nov. 1881. **15** Moody & Hawkins (eds), *Florence Arnold-Forster's Irish journal*, p. 305. **16** NAI CSO RP 1881/38495

After the inquest, RM Franks attended at Craughwell, where the four prisoners were brought before him. SI Bell charged them with being concerned with the murder and asked for a remand to enable him to produce further evidence. Franks granted the request and they were remanded to Ardrahan Petty Sessions on 7 November. Franks believed there was a sufficient charge capable of proof against James Morrissey because, when he was arrested on the night of the murder, five bullets and percussion caps were found in his possession. Franks requested that RM William Morris Reade, Galway, should hear the case with him because none of the local magistrates were willing to attend. John Newell was released because of lack of evidence against him. In view of his leadership position of the local Fenians, it is somewhat surprising that he was released, but the police must have been unaware of his Fenian affiliations.

At the hearing in Ardrahan, a further remand was granted and at the next court appearance in Gort the sessional crown solicitor, Mr William French Henderson, applied for another remand because SI Alan Bell swore that he had received important information that he believed would further implicate the prisoners. Bell also stated that 'from the terrorism which prevailed in the locality of the murder, his efforts to investigate properly the facts of the case were much retarded'. Two further remands were granted despite the strong protests of the solicitor for the defence who pointed out that no evidence had been presented to inculpate his clients.[17] Franks was also embarrassed that 'not a particle of evidence incriminating the prisoners had as yet been produced'. Finally, at Gort Courthouse on 25 November, he heard evidence from six witnesses and decided that a probable case of guilt had been established against James Morrissey, who was committed for trial at Galway winter assizes. Patrick Morrissey and Thomas Cunniffe were discharged but were immediately re-arrested under the Protection of Person and Property (Ireland) Act of 1881 and charged with being accessories to murder. RM Franks complimented Bell in an extravagant fashion, referring to his 'untiring zeal and intelligence that obtained under the greatest difficulties of widespread terrorism, a train of such minute circumstantial evidence sufficient to send Morrissey for trial'. The possession of bullets and percussion caps was the main evidence adduced against him and Franks ignored the testimony given that the ammunition had been in the Morrisseys' house for a considerable time and that James had surrendered his gun when the Arms Act was passed in March 1881. Evidence had also been given that both Morrisseys were in a neighbour's house at the time of the murder. That Franks ignored this evidence is not surprising, because alibi evidence was commonly regarded as suspect and to be expected in close-knit communities intent on concealing the perpetrators of crime. The trial of James Morrissey at the winter assizes was adjourned at the request of Mr Frost, the prisoner's solicitor,[18] and when he came to trial in March

in 1881/41874.   17 NAI CSO RP 1881/40261 in 1881/41874.   18 *Galway Vindicator*, 21 Dec. 1881.

1882 at the spring assizes he was discharged by proclamation.[19] The crown had clearly decided that the 'minute circumstantial evidence' collected by SI Alan Bell and lauded by RM Franks was insufficient to proceed with the prosecution. On 15 May 1882, a warrant for Morrissey's arrest under the Coercion Act was issued,[20] but there is no record of an arrest. He emigrated to America after the trial and died there as a result of a shooting incident.

Great excitement was generated in the locality at the various court appearances and, in a report to the under secretary, Mr William French Henderson referred to the conduct of the mob at Gort and particularly at Ardrahan and Craughwell railway stations during the transport of the prisoners. 'Cheering and hooting prevailed, every sympathy with crime was exhibited; and I can hardly fancy anything more calculated to enlist popular feeling in favour of murder and in hostility to order than the scenes which were observable'. He blamed the railway company for not excluding the mob from the stations.[21]

LOCAL EVENTS IN THE AFTERMATH OF THE DOHERTY KILLING

The boycott of the Dohertys continued after the killing, and on 19 November a slate was put up at John Doherty's house bearing the word 'grabber' and a drawing of a coffin. Later, he received another notice threatening him with Peter's fate if he remained in Walter Bourke's employment.[22] Throughout the month of November 1881, the police investigations continued under the direction of SIs French and Bell. On 13 November, a third member of the Morrissey family, Thomas, aged twenty-one, was arrested under the Coercion Act and detained in Dundalk Jail. A party of police led by Sergeant Patrick Keehan searched the house of Patrick Finnegan in Aggard on 16 November and found a percussion cap of an old pattern in the pocket of a pair of trousers.[23] On 30 November, it was proposed that a reward be offered and the attorney general's opinion was sought.

There was an interesting development at Christmas 1881, when James Regan, steward for Walter Bourke, suddenly departed for America. Regan had become extremely worried by remarks the Dohertys were making that connected him with the killing and he decided to emigrate before the police could take any action. There are no reports of his departure in the chief secretary's office records, but a newspaper account claimed that he left with £400 belonging to Walter Bourke.[24] The police believed that Regan had written threatening letters with the intention of alarming Bourke about the dangerous state of the area. Regan hoped that this would keep Bourke away from Rahasane House so that he

19 *Freeman's Journal*, 1 Apr. 1882. 20 NAI CSO RP 1882/22595. 21 NAI CSO RP 1881/41869. 22 NLI Parnell Special Commission, i, p. 512, Evidence of Alan Bell. 23 *Tuam News*, 25 July 1884. 24 *Freeman's Journal*, 7 Jan. 1882.

would have a free hand managing the estate. After Regan's departure, the police searched his house and found several boycotting notices similar to those recently posted in the district. They arrested Regan's son Patrick, who was aged about fourteen years, and sent him to Galway Jail.[25] He was brought before the spring assizes in Galway and indicted for writing a threatening letter to Patrick Raftery, an employee of Walter Bourke. The young boy was bound over to be of good behaviour on security of £100.[26] At a later stage, Raftery was to play an important role as an informer in the Doherty case.

THE ARREST OF PATRICK FINNEGAN AND OTHER SUSPECTS

Kate Doherty claimed that she had expressed suspicions of Finnegan's involvement in the murder to her parents and SI Alan Bell, because she thought she recognized him at the scene.[27] RM Henry Arthur Blake proposed Finnegan's arrest on 3 March 1882,[28] and the Coercion Act warrant was issued on 12 April. The reasons cited for his arrest were that he was 'a known boycotter' and that Kate Doherty thought he was one of the assassins.[29] In the early hours of 17 April, a party of police led by SI Bell burst in the door, ransacked the house and abused the family. Finnegan was committed to Galway Jail, charged as an accessory to murder.[30] The Loughrea correspondent of the *Tuam News* commented:

> of all the mysteries that have occurred in this district, this is the most mysterious. Mr Finnegan's respectability is quite sufficient to shield him in the mind of every honest born individual ... from the breath of any such suspicion. The charge is a sham ... and shows how the officers of law and order in Craughwell are doing their duty.[31]

On 17 July 1882, as part of the continuing investigations of the Doherty killing, Special Resident Magistrate Clifford Lloyd led a strong force of police to Craughwell and arrested six men, namely Thomas Connolly (Mannin), John Connaire (Caheradine), Thomas Pendergast (Carrigan), Michael Connolly (Ballywinna), Michael Fogarty (Shanbally) and Thomas Joyce (Ballywinna).[32] At the hearing before RM Byrne, Constable Judge claimed that they were all members of a secret society. They were charged with being accessories to the murder of Peter Doherty. By the time they were leaving the police barracks, a large crowd had gathered to protest about their arrests, but a man called Ryan pleaded

25 *Freeman's Journal*, 7 Jan. 1882. 26 *Galway Express*, 1 Apr. 1882. 27 NAI CRF misc. 1903/396, witness deposition of Kate Doherty, Mar. 1883. 28 NAI CSO RP 1882/11672. 29 NAI Protection of Person and Property (Ireland) Act 1881, iv. 30 NAI Protection of Person and Property (Ireland) Act 1881, List of persons arrested. 31 *Tuam News*, 21 Apr. 1882. 32 *Tuam News*, 21 July 1882.

for calm and advised the crowd to depart peacefully. The correspondent of the *Tuam News* claimed that the district had been comparatively peaceful until the passing of the Coercion Act. 'With its introduction, oppression was stimulated, evictions began and outrage was the result, leading to its disturbed state'.[33]

In mid-August, the fifteen prisoners from the Craughwell area were released and their return home was an occasion of joyous celebration. The windows were illuminated and bonfires blazed while a large crowd conveyed them to their homes in Carrigan, Ballywinna and Derryhoyle.[34] At this stage, there had been no prosecutions in court in relation to the Doherty killing, but for three of the 'suspects', Patrick Finnegan, Thomas Joyce and Michael Connolly, the release proved to be only a short reprieve.

Following the discharge and triumphant home-coming of the 'suspects', there was no lessening of the activities of SI Alan Bell, Constable Redington and the other police attached to Craughwell Barracks who were investigating the Doherty murder case. Attention was next focused on the 'suspects' who were present at the Irish National League meeting at Ballymana in December 1882. The meeting had been proclaimed and the police attempted to disperse the crowd. Afterwards, SI Bell submitted thirty-five names of those attending, including Finnegan, Connolly and Fogarty, who were described as having bad or very bad characters.[35] A few days later, thirty-three warrants for arrest were issued and Patrick Finnegan, Michael Connolly and Michael Fogarty and thirty others were sentenced to three weeks imprisonment for riotous assembly (see below, appendix 2). While they were in Galway Jail, there were reports of intensive police activities in the Craughwell area and it was believed that the police officers were asking questions and trying to frighten people into becoming informers.[36] In addition, the prisoners had the sobering experience of entering Galway Jail a few days after the hanging of three Maamtrasna prisoners and were inmates when Patrick and Thomas Higgins and Michael Flynn were executed for another agrarian crime, the killing of Joseph Huddy and his grandson near Lough Mask, Co. Mayo.

Finnegan, Connolly and Fogarty were released from Galway Jail on 21 January 1883, and they walked home to Craughwell.[37]

DRAMATIC DEVELOPMENTS IN THE DOHERTY CASE

Five days after their return home, Finnegan, Connolly and Fogarty were arrested again, along with John Conway (Grenage) and Thomas Joyce (Ballywinna), and transferred to Galway Jail. It quickly became known that the

---

33 *Tuam News*, 21 July 1882.   **34** *Tuam News*, 8 Sept. 1882.   **35** NAI CSO RP 1883/153.   **36** *Tuam News*, 26 Jan. 1883.   **37** Ibid.

arrests were made on the basis of an information[38] given to the police by a man called Patrick Raftery, who worked as a herd at Rahasane House.[39] Raftery was placed under the protection of the police at Athenry police station, while continuing to help with their enquiries. In his case, there was no need to frighten him into giving evidence, as baser, pecuniary motives rather than fear were the spur. Another man, Nedeen Callanan from Killeeneen, was also interviewed in Athenry police station because he was suspected of 'knowing something'. After several days interrogation, 'he was given up as a bad job'.[40] Raftery was sent to Galway and was placed under the protection of Constable R. Hughes, who purchased a coat, trousers, vest and shirt for him. On 6 February, Head Constable I. Hensey wrote to Dublin Castle stating that there was no authority for the support of Raftery.[41] However, Clifford Lloyd acknowledged that he had given authority for support because he was 'a most important witness in a serious murder case'.[42]

THE ARREST OF MICHAEL MULDOWNEY

The arrest of Constable Michael Muldowney followed on 10 February.[43] Muldowney was a native of Ballygeeher, Co. Leitrim, who joined the RIC in 1876. The following year he was posted to Craughwell, where he was engaged in patrols at Doherty's house during the boycott. In 1881, he was transferred to protection duty at Rahasane House following death threats to Walter Bourke. In addition to protecting Bourke, he also had the duty of guarding James Regan, Bourke's steward, who lived close by in the Garden House. On the morning after the killing of Peter Doherty, SI Alan Bell asked Muldowney about Regan's whereabouts on the previous night and Muldowney said he had been with him all that evening. At that stage, Muldowney was unaware that Regan was suspected of involvement in the murder and unwittingly incriminated himself. At the end of November, three weeks after the killing, Muldowney was transferred from Rahasane to Craughwell and then to Dublin, where he was placed on detective duties until his recall to Galway on 3 January 1883. His recall was a consequence of Raftery's information, but at that stage Muldowney did not know he was suspected of involvement in the killing. SRM Clifford Lloyd, RM A.N. Brady, HC Wynne and District Inspector John D. Phillips questioned Muldowney intensively and without caution, the final sessions taking place at Clifford Lloyd's residence in Lenaboy.

On 10 February, Michael Muldowney was arrested by HC Wynne and

---

38 'An information' is a statement establishing the charge. It was taken in the absence of the accused.   39 *Western News*, 10 Feb. 1883.   40 *Tuam News*, 9 Feb. 1883.   41 NAI CSO RP 1883/13481, Hensey to IG, 6 Feb. 1883.   42 NAI CSO RP 1883/13481, Clifford Lloyd to under secretary, 25 Feb. 1883.   43 *Galway Express*, 17 Feb. 1883.

charged before RM A.N. Brady that 'with others he wilfully and feloniously murdered Peter Doherty Junior'. On being charged and after caution, he made the following statement:

> I deny the charge. I have never mixed myself up with a band of Land League assassins yet. I have been placed in confidence and trust since the occurrence and I have never broken it. I have been on detection duty since 25 November 1881 until 23 January 1883 and have always done my duty to the best of my ability. I have served my queen and country up to this day honestly.[44]

In fact, Michael Muldowney was reared on a medium sized farm in reasonable comfort and the family was not associated with any rebellious activity. On his maternal side, his uncle Michael Mahon was a retired RIC sergeant. During the trials, the admissibility of the earlier statements made by Muldowney regarding Regan would be hotly contested because he was not formally cautioned before making them.

THE DEPOSITIONS OF WITNESSES[45]

Following the six arrests, a series of magisterial investigations took place and the sworn depositions of the principal witnesses are contained in a brief prepared for the solicitor general in June 1883 by Crown Solicitor Thomas D. Farrell, prior to the commencement of the trials. The brief also contained an engineer's map of the locality of the crime and the surrounding areas (fig. 4, p. 41). It is fortunate that these documents survive, because there is no record of statements made prior to the sworn depositions and there are no transcripts of the evidence given at the trials.

Statements by Patrick Raftery
Patrick Raftery gave his first information under oath before RM A.N. Brady on 17 February 1883.[46] He said that on the day of the murder he had seen James Regan and Michael Muldowney leaving Rahasane House and travelling to Craughwell in a car. On the same afternoon, Raftery also went to Craughwell in order to buy whiskey to ease the pain of a toothache. He said he spent an hour and a half in Craughwell before walking home. When he reached Aggard Bridge (Donohue's bridge), he saw a group of eight men down the boreen beside the

---

44 NAI CRF misc. 484/03, in Misc. 396/03. Petition for release prepared by Solicitor Richard Jennings, Oct. 1885.   45 A deposition was a written and sworn statement taken at an inquiry in the presence of the accused.   46 NAI CSO RP, Misc. 396/03. Brief prepared for the crown by T.D. Farrell, crown solicitor, June 1883.

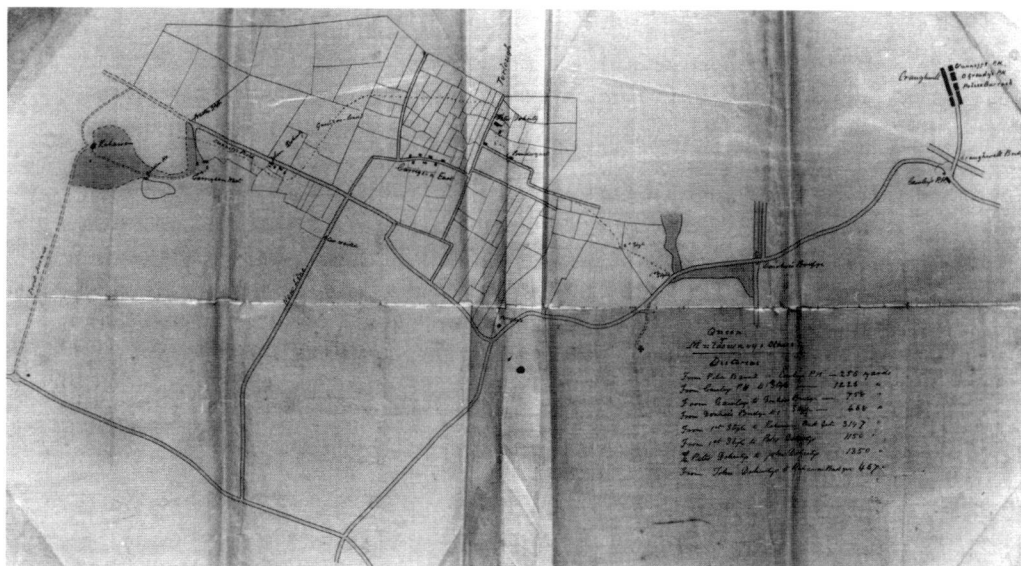

4 Map of the locality of Peter Doherty's house. Some distances given on the map, but not legible in this reproduction: 'from police barracks to Cawley's public house – 256 yards; from Cawley's public house to first stile – 1,226 yards; from Cawley's public house to Aggard Bridge [Donohue's bridge] – 758 yards; from Donohue's bridge to first stile – 468 yards; from first stile to Peter Doherty's – 1,150 yards; from Donohue's bridge to Rahasane back gate – 3,147 yards' (National Archives of Ireland Convict Reference File, Miscellaneous 1903; image reproduced courtesy of the Director of the National Archives of Ireland).

bridge and one of the group, James Regan, approached and told him to 'go on out of that'. Raftery identified Finnegan and Fogarty at the bridge before he walked along the road as far as the stile that gave access to the shortcut through the fields to Carrigan. He crossed the wall opposite the stile and observed the group of men approaching the stile. He saw Regan carrying a gun and named Finnegan, Fogarty, Joyce, Connolly, Conway and Muldowney in the group, but he claimed he was unable to identify the remaining person. The men crossed the stile and walked towards Carrigan. Raftery continued along the road towards Rahasane and before he reached it he heard shots in the direction of Peter Doherty's. He continued to the back gate of Rahasane House and while sitting on a stone he heard three or four shots near John Doherty's and shortly afterwards he claimed he saw Regan running across Cunniffe's lawn field going towards Rahasane. There were two others running in the field below Regan but Raftery did not recognize them.

A second statement by Raftery, a week later, contained more precise information regarding the departure time of Regan and Muldowney from Rahasane House, which he said occurred between 4pm and 5pm and he also said that his own return from Craughwell occurred between 7pm and 8pm. The later time provided a better linkage with the time of the Doherty shooting and other evidence yet to appear. In naming the people at the stile, Raftery claimed that Regan and Muldowney had guns and Fogarty had something like a gun, whereas in the first statement only Regan had a gun. There was a discrepancy also in placing the men running in Cunniffe's field above rather than below Regan.

It is not known precisely when Raftery began to give information to the police, but it was probably in the latter part of 1882, and the identification of Muldowney and Regan in the murder party was a sufficient incentive to order Muldowney's return to Galway to face interrogation. As far as the crown was concerned, the association of Muldowney and Regan was a key element, and later the attorney general was to refer to Regan as 'the leader, the person who planned it and a villain of the most awful and desperate type'.[47] Not a shred of evidence was produced to justify these allegations.

Statements by the Doherty family
The next sworn statement was that of Peter Doherty's sister, Kate, in which she purported to identify one of the men at the murder scene: 'I saw the figure of a man standing at the other side of the yard wall. The man saw me and made off as fast as if I was going to shoot him. I had not sufficient time to identify the man; he got away too quickly, and I had not a dry eye at the time'. Despite the obvious inability to identify the person, she went on to state: 'judging from the view I got of the man, I believed the man I saw there at the wall was Finnegan, and next day when my mind was not so distracted, I came to believe this'. She then made a strange comment under cross-examination: 'my belief that it was Finnegan I saw that night was not made up by what I saw that night, I had something to help it'. On further questioning, this transpired to be a remark made by her brother two nights before the murder, but she did not reveal the nature of the remark. Thereafter, this incredibly vague identification of Finnegan was regarded as important independent testimony at the trials.

Other points made by the Dohertys concerned the furious barking of the dog at the murder scene, an insinuation that Muldowney was not a friend, and John Doherty's claim that he thought he heard Regan's voice when the shots were fired at his house. 'It fitted in my heart' that the voice was that of Regan.

At the magisterial enquiry on 17 March, Constable Redington said he had ascertained that information of an important nature would shortly be forthcoming. It was not long before Jack Moran, a tailor from Killeeneen, delivered the corroboration.

47 *Tuam News*, 18 July 1884.

Depositions of John (Jack) Moran

Jack Moran presented himself as an approver – the term applied to someone who participates in a crime and afterwards becomes an informer. It had long been suspected in the Craughwell area that SI Alan Bell and Constable Redington were endeavouring to procure informers. The emergence of Moran as an approver immediately raised the question of collusion between Raftery and Moran under the tuition of Bell and Redington. It would also explain the intriguing failure of Raftery to identify the eighth person in the alleged shooting party, namely Moran. If he had identified him at an earlier stage, Moran would have been arrested and charged with the murder along with the other prisoners.

The first deposition was made before RM A.N. Brady at Ennis Courthouse on 20 April 1883. John (Jack) Moran was formerly a soldier in the British Army and, ten years previously, had been given a dishonourable discharge. The reasons given for this were insubordination, drunkenness and general misconduct, and when he was leaving the army he was branded with the initials 'BC', meaning 'bad character'.[48] In his statement, Moran claimed that a year previously Michael Fogarty had sworn him into the 'Patriotic Brotherhood'.[49] On the day of the murder of Peter Doherty, he claimed to have left Killeeneen at approximately 7pm and walked to Craughwell, where he met Fogarty, Joyce, Connolly and Conway. Fogarty said to Moran 'you must come with them to shoot the Dohertys, if not we'll boycott you'. When they entered Cawley's public house, they met Finnegan who joined them. Shortly afterwards, Regan and Muldowney came in and they had some drink together. On leaving Cawley's, Regan, Fogarty and either Joyce or Finnegan (Moran was not sure who) went as passengers on the car and he walked with Conway and Connolly as far as Aggard Bridge, where they met the others. In the boreen beside the bridge, Regan gave each of them a gun except Conway and Muldowney, who had his own gun. This information was at variance with the evidence given by Raftery, who said, in his second deposition, that only Regan and Muldowney had guns and Fogarty had something like a gun. It is also flawed on the grounds that he should certainly remember whichever individual (either Joyce or Finnegan) did not travel on the car and who would have walked with Moran, Conway and Connolly on the road.

At the murder scene, Moran placed himself with Fogarty, Connolly and Finnegan behind the wall opposite the house, and Regan, Muldowney and Joyce in the haggard. Conway released the horse from the stable, and called out: 'Peter, your horse is loose'. The first shots he claimed came from the haggard and Peter Doherty fell. The other shots were fired as he was falling or after he fell. Moran may have been trying to ensure his own innocence of the murder by placing himself in front of the house with the fatal shot coming from the haggard.

---

48 *Tuam News*, 25 July 1884.   49 The 'Patriotic Brotherhood' was another name applied to the Fenians.

However, the post-mortem (see above, p. 34) showed that the fatal shot entered at the left shoulder and was, therefore, discharged from behind the wall and not from the haggard. Forensic analysis at the time was almost non-existent and the engineer did not visit the site until nineteen months after the shooting. At that late stage, he traced the bullets that had entered the house. One of them had come from directly in front of the house, and the other at an angle consistent with a trajectory from the haggard.

After the shooting, Moran claimed that they all ran away towards Rahasane turlough and they crossed the fields to John Doherty's, where three or four shots were fired (fig. 4, p. 41). They had reloaded their guns on the way, but Moran claimed that he did not reload because he had not fired any shots. He further claimed that he saw Regan and another man going towards Rahasane. He then gave his gun to Fogarty and ran away through the fields to Craughwell, where he had a drink in Cunniffe's public house before going home.

On 21 June, SI Alan Bell gave a second information, sworn by Moran, to CS Thomas Farrell. In a marginal note, Farrell commented that the attorney general strongly disapproved of this second statement, pointing out that in its opening passage it contradicted the first deposition taken on 20 April. Moran now described a meeting with Fogarty, Joyce, Connolly and Finnegan on the day before the murder and said that Fogarty told him he would be wanted in Craughwell on the following night. He then said he did not go home at all that night and was in Craughwell all the next day, having previously maintained that he had gone from his house in Killeeneen to Craughwell on the night of the murder. In the second statement, Moran did not refer to Muldowney having his own gun and did not mention that Regan ran towards Rahasane. At the trials, the defence counsel complained that they were never given sight of this contradicting document.

Statement of James Fox

James Fox, an ex-sergeant in the Queen's Hussars and now coachman and servant at Rahasane House, swore the final deposition. Fox said that Constable Lee was on duty as guard in the policemen's room on the day of the murder and that Muldowney was out a good deal. Muldowney was in the habit of keeping company with Regan, being constantly in Regan's office, and Fox remembered them going out shooting together. Before he had his supper, at about 8pm, Fox went to the policemen's room and found Constable Lee there by himself. Afterwards, he went to bed and at 10.15pm was woken by Lee, who told him about the murder. When Fox returned to the policemen's room, he found Lee there alone until Muldowney and Regan came in. Fox reported that Regan said that '[we] will all be shot soon' and asked Fox for a gun. Because he looked so white and frightened, Fox gave him a gun. They all went to Regan's house, where Regan offered them whiskey and Fox and Lee accepted the drink. Fox brought Lee back to Rahasane House and Muldowney went out to search the neighbourhood. During the search, Muldowney and Constable Laing arrested Thomas Cunniffe, the former tenant of the boycotted land, and Muldowney also visited the Dohertys' house.

The evidence indicating Muldowney's absence from the policemen's room and comments on his close links with Regan were considered to be of such importance that Fox was maintained as a crown witness until the trials were abandoned in March 1885.

Recruitment of informers and treatment of crown witnesses
During the Land War, there was a marked increase in agrarian crime and consequently a greatly increased workload on the already hard-pressed police and the law officers of the crown. In addition, there was often a lack of coordination between the investigating magistrates and the crown solicitors who prosecuted the cases in court.[50] The detective branch of the RIC had been established recently, but it was poorly staffed. The task of obtaining information about crime was a formidable one in tightly knit communities intent on protecting the perpetrators. Sums of money were allocated for the recruitment of informers, and monetary reward was also the motivation for many of the approvers who had been or claimed to have been involved in crime but offered to give evidence in exchange for immunity from prosecution. Cultivated, protected and finally 'disposed of', the crown witnesses were an important part of the government's strategy for the procurement of convictions in a climate of distrust and lack of respect for the law. The system of protection for the crown witnesses involved police guards, the provision of accommodation and clothes for the informers and their families and regular financial support. Vaughan adverted to the observations of William Thorpe Porter on the treatment of crown witnesses.[51] Porter referred to two houses in Ship Street where crown witnesses were lodged. He claimed that

> the crown witnesses were accustomed to have their evidence rehearsed before an amateur judge, an improvised jury and a couple of supposed counsel, one to prosecute and the other to defend. If a case failed, the witnesses were instructed as to their deficiencies, either in manner or matter; and they were drilled to avoid omissions of any nature calculated to weaken their testimony.

Having discovered this centre of excellence, Porter made such representations to the executive as produced the suppression of the Ship Street establishment.

---

50 For a detailed discussion, see Stephen Andrew Ball, *Policing the Land War* (London, 2000), chs 8, 9. 51 Frank Thorpe Porter, *Gleanings and reminiscences* (Dublin, 1876), pp 197–8, quoted in W.E. Vaughan, *Murder trials in Ireland, 1836–1914* (Dublin, 2009), p. 78.

However, it is possible that similar practises continued in the later establishments in Ballybough and Kingscourt House, Clontarf.

E.G. Jenkinson[52] revealed the cost of the system in a letter to Lord Spencer in 1884. He stated that the amount paid for information since June 1882 was £6,500, and rewards for witnesses, prisoners who became informers in trials and emigration expenses were £2,726. The total cost was £14,250 and Jenkinson requested a budget of £20,000 for 1884–5.[53]

52 Edward G. Jenkinson, head of Dublin Castle intelligence section.   53 Peter Gordon, *The Red Earl* (Northampton, 1981), letter 339, p. 262, Jenkinson to Spencer, 15 Jan. 1884.

4 The trials of Michael Muldowney

INTRODUCTION

At the magisterial enquiry before RM Lyster, on 29 March, the six prisoners (Finnegan, Connolly, Fogarty, Conway, Joyce and Muldowney) arrested in relation to the murder of Peter Doherty were formally remanded for trial at Galway summer assizes.[1] An application for bail, pending his trial, was made on Muldowney's behalf before the court of the queen's bench. In his affidavit, Muldowney swore that he was 'wholly innocent of the charge', but the application was turned down.[2]

The attorney general was allowed, under sections 4 and 6 of the Prevention of Crime (Ireland) Act of 1882, to change the venue of trials and also to have the trials heard before special juries. This power was widely availed of by the crown in trials of agrarian crimes and had resulted in a significant improvement in the number of successful prosecutions. Whereas the detection rate for agrarian crime remained low, the success of the change of venue and special juries provisions can be gauged from the fact that during the winter assizes of 1882, 52 per cent of cases resulted in conviction.[3] When change of venue cases were analyzed separately, the conviction rate was 79 per cent. In the case of the Craughwell prisoners, the change of venue from Galway to Sligo and the trials before special juries played a significant part in the outcome of the trials.

SLIGO SUMMER ASSIZES, JULY 1883

When Judge James Murphy (fig. 6, p. 49)[4] addressed the Sligo grand jury on 9 July 1883, he did so in the manner he had become accustomed to as a leading crown prosecutor. Referring to the Doherty killing, he said that the grand jury 'would have no doubt ... judging from the depositions before him, an opportunity of seeing that a very gross and brutal murder was perpetrated on that night

---

1 *Tuam News*, 30 Mar. 1883. 2 *Galway Vindicator*, 25 Apr. 1883. 3 NAI CSO RP 1891/ 28047, memo by Rt Hon. John Naish on Sections 4–6 of the Prevention of Crime (Ireland) Act 1882. 4 James Murphy (1823–1901). A native of Limerick, he became QC in 1866 and was appointed a justice to the common pleas division in 1883. He was crown prosecutor at the state trial of Parnell and others, the trial of the Invincibles for the Phoenix Park murders and also at the Maamtrasna trial, for which he received a fee of £485. He was a son-in-law of Judge Keogh and it was believed he assisted Keogh to write the infamous judgment, lasting nine hours, delivered by Keogh at the trial following the 1872 Galway election. See BL Spencer papers, 76854, Spencer to Gladstone, 7 June 1882. Spencer also commented: 'as a lawyer, I hear he is not as good as others, but would make an excellent judge'.

5 Sligo assize court,
The Graphic, 6 Dec.
1879.

by a large gang of assassins'. The tone of his remarks suggests that he had already made his mind up regarding the guilt of the 'gang of assassins'. However, the case was not heard on that occasion and it was adjourned to the winter assizes.

SLIGO WINTER ASSIZES, 1883

The Doherty case was listed for hearing before Judge William O'Brien at the Sligo winter assizes. In addition, the Letterfrack and Linton cases were listed and a total of twenty-two prisoners were transferred, under heavy escort, from Galway to Sligo for the trials.[5] When the Doherty case was called, Sergeant Robinson QC asked for an adjournment. This was granted on the grounds that

5 *Galway Vindicator*, 1 Dec. 1883.

6 Judge James Murphy, from Matthias McDonnell Bodkin, *Recollections of an Irish judge* (New York, 1915).

a material witness had gone to America. The witness was Constable Lee, who, according to Muldowney, had been in his company on the night of the murder. Two policemen from Craughwell were sent to America on two occasions in an attempt to persuade Lee to return, but he refused.[6] The absence of Lee was to have an important effect on the outcome of the trials.

Following the adjournment, the accused men remained in prison but the police investigations continued in the Craughwell area, led as before by the promoted DI, Alan Bell, and Sergeant Redington. Allegations of harassment were made in a newspaper account that also claimed that bribes were being offered to potential witnesses for the prosecution. One of those approached was Margaret Raftery, wife of the informer, but she refused and instead she became a witness for the defence. The article stated that Redington paid numerous visits

6 NAI CSO RP 1885/5161, I. Hensey to CI J. Byrne, 12 Dec. 1883.

to the home of Ellen Conway, widowed mother of the prisoner John Conway.
Redington repeatedly reminded her of the proof that he possessed of her son's
guilt and that he would be hanged. The paper claimed that as a result she became
mentally ill and was unable to care for herself. On 24 January 1884, she was
removed to Loughrea Workhouse, where she died seven days later.

THE FIRST TRIAL OF MICHAEL MULDOWNEY,
SLIGO SPRING ASSIZES, MARCH 1884

The first trial of Muldowney commenced on 7 March 1884 before Justice James
Murphy at the Sligo spring assizes.[7] In the prosecution team were Sergeant
Robinson QC, Mr Francis Nolan QC and Mr F. le Poer Trench QC, instructed
by Thomas D. Farrell CS. The defence counsel was made up of Mr John Stritch
QC and Mr Taylor QC, instructed by Richard Jennings, Gort. The jury
members were Captain G. Gethin (chairman), C. Hall, Alexander Petrie, J.
Shaw, William Barrett, John O'Donnell, Edward Williams, R. Gorman, John
Hunter, Henry Shaw, Alex Gillmor and H. Robinson.[8]

    In his opening address, Sergeant Robinson QC gave a muddled account of the
events on the night of the murder that in many respects was at variance with the
depositions of the Dohertys, Raftery, Moran and others. Robinson referred
tendentiously to Regan and Muldowney absconding to Craughwell in a car with
guns. He asserted that Sub Constable Corcoran 'will prove' that he saw
Muldowney and Regan drive to Cawley's public house. Corcoran's evidence in
the first trial is not reported, but in the second trial he merely referred to
Muldowney and Regan crossing over the bridge at Cawley's, between 5pm and
6pm, without saying that they stopped there. Robinson stated that Moran, the
approver, would prove that Muldowney with a number of others assembled by
order of the 'Head Centre Regan'. In fact, the Fenian Head Centre for the
barony of Dunkellin was John Newell, who was arrested for a brief period after
the killing and was released without charge because of the lack of evidence to
link him with the crime. However, Robinson's statement reflected the contention
of the crown that Regan was the chief organizer of the killing of Peter Doherty
and if Muldowney was in his company that night, as he admitted, then he was
also implicated. Robinson then asserted that the two men who were seen running
across Cunniffe's field with Regan were Muldowney and Thomas Cunniffe. If
that was so, why was Cunniffe not charged with the murder? He was an early
suspect, who was arrested on the night of the murder by Constable Muldowney.
During the initial investigations, RM Franks produced no evidence of
Cunniffe's involvement in the murder and he was merely detained as a suspect

---

7 *Irish Times*, 8 Mar. 1884. 8 *Sligo Champion*, 15 Mar. 1884.

under the Protection of Person and Property (Ireland) Act of 1881. Robinson also referred to Muldowney's statement on the morning after the murder – that he was with Regan between 7pm and 9pm on the previous night. Initially, this was viewed as an alibi for Regan that allowed him to emigrate to America, but when Raftery delivered his story, naming Muldowney and Regan in the shooting party, it acquired a more sinister significance.

The evidence given by the main witnesses was similar to their depositions, but for the first time witnesses for the defence were heard.[9] Margaret Raftery, wife of the informer, said that her husband was at home and did not go out again following his return from Craughwell soon after nightfall. 'He was very ill with a toothache and remained all night lying by the fire with his head on a pillow rising up now and again to walk about the floor'. John Healy stated that he met Jack Moran, the approver, who was a relation of his, at 8pm. Moran was very drunk and he was going towards Killeeneen in the opposite direction to the murder. He was certain of the time because when he reached Craughwell post office, the clock showed 8.10pm. One of the witnesses gave contradictory accounts of Regan's movements on the night of the murder. This was Mary Forde, a servant in Regan's house, who said on one occasion that Regan came home from Craughwell at about 5pm, and on another that she did not know what time he arrived home. She also conceded that she did not tell the truth to RM A.N. Brady because she did not understand the reason for the questions and was afraid of incriminating anyone. At the trial, she said that Regan remained in the house all night and Muldowney came to the house about nightfall. It was unfortunate for Muldowney's defence that the young girl, exposed to the intimidatory atmosphere of magisterial investigations, gave some contradictory statements that resulted in doubts being cast on her credibility as a witness.

For the prosecution, Mrs Maria Moran, wife of Jack Moran, swore that her husband came home at about 11pm and that he often came home late and drunk. Mr Somerville, an engineer, said that the crown solicitor spoke to him about the case for the first time on 22 June 1883 (nineteen months after the murder). He said that he examined the doors and traced two bullets; one came from opposite the door and the other came in a slanting direction.[10] Sergeant Redington showed him the position Raftery claimed to have occupied behind the wall at the stile but Somerville was unable to see the stile from the point indicated. Two days later he returned with Redington, who identified a different position. However, Somerville thought the view of the stile was 'about the same from both positions'. Contemporary examination of the scene confirms the difficulty because the ground falls away sharply immediately behind the wall.[11]

The case for the crown relied mainly on the evidence of Moran and Raftery, and Moran claimed that Regan and Muldowney were the principal organizers

9 *Irish Times*, 10 Mar. 1884. 10 *Sligo Champion*, 15 Mar. 1884. 11 Observations of the present author and Maura Lyons, Aug. 2007.

and directors of the attack. The crown also claimed that Muldowney admitted
to the investigating magistrates that he provided an alibi for Regan, even though
he was aware that Regan was the author of threatening letters.[12]

Muldowney's counsel, Mr Stritch QC, cross-examined Moran, who denied
that he was drunk on the evening of the murder and when asked if he was
branded BC,[13] Moran said 'I am not'. Stritch asked the question again and
this time Moran answered 'I am'. He then asked Moran if he had denied the
charge 'a moment ago in the presence of the jury'. Moran replied 'No'. Stritch
called on the jury not to believe Moran or Raftery and not to convict Muldowney
on the basis of statements made, without caution, before SRM Clifford Lloyd
and RM A.N. Brady. He had earlier objected to the admissibility of the statements, but was overruled by Judge Murphy.[14] In the trial of Finnegan in July
1884, Brady's statement was ruled inadmissible by the same judge. In the
absence of transcripts of the questioning of Muldowney before he was charged,
it is not possible to decide if the statements were voluntary or made in response
to a question. It would be expected that an experienced lawyer like James
Murphy would be aware of the distinction between the two conditions
governing admissibility of statements, yet he gave contradictory rulings in
separate trials.

Judge Murphy summed up the evidence for more than three hours. Captain
Gethin, foreman of the jury, returned to ask about Muldowney's ammunition
and DI Alan Bell responded that it was examined 'a few days later and was found
to be perfectly correct.'[15] After the killing, a story had circulated in the
Craughwell area to the effect that Muldowney had been playing cards in the
house of a family called Morless in Carrigan and that his gun was taken without
his knowledge and used in the murder. Supporting evidence for this claim has
not been found.

After two hours deliberation, the jury foreman said that there was no possibility of agreement and the trial was adjourned to the summer assizes. A press
report suggested that the jury, which 'comprised a large number of the resident
gentry of the county, [was] divided in the proportion of nine for acquittal, two
for a conviction and one who was unable to reach any conclusion on the
evidence'.[16]

In letters to Divisional Magistrate Andrew Reed after the trial, DI Alan Bell
commented that a most formidable case had been made by the crown and Judge
Murphy had charged the jury very strongly against the prisoner. Bell said that

---

12 *Freeman's Journal*, 8 Mar. 1884.   13 BC stands for 'bad character' and Moran was branded
thus in 1877 when he was dishonourably discharged from the 1st Battalion of the 9th Regiment.
14 In his book *Murder trials in Ireland, 1836–1914*, W.E. Vaughan cites the opinions of Levinge
and O'Connor on admissibility of statements. A voluntary statement by the accused is admissible
but a statement made in response to a question is not (p. 75).   15 *Sligo Champion*, 15 Mar. 1884.
16 *Freeman's Journal*, 10 Mar. 1884.

the jury was equally divided and the foreman told him that 'it was the fact of Muldowney being a policeman that prevented them finding him guilty'. Bell also thought it was a mistake not to try one of the civilian prisoners first as there would be every chance of a conviction.[17] A re-trial was adjourned, as were the trials of the other five prisoners, and Mr McDonnell Bodkin QC,[18] who represented them, referred to the great hardship his clients had suffered and requested that the crown 'secure the evidence of the witnesses who had left the country'.[19]

THE SECOND TRIAL OF MICHAEL MULDOWNEY,
SLIGO SUMMER ASSIZES, JULY 1884

The second trial of Muldowney began on 14 July 1884 before Judge James Murphy. Muldowney was described as 'a handsome, neatly dressed young man' who displayed 'a pleasing and unperturbed demeanour during the trial.'[20] There was also a comment on the appearance of the two crown witnesses, Raftery and Moran; both were well dressed and Moran 'sported a watch and chain'. The jury was a matter of concern for the defence because it was composed of ten Protestants, five of whom were landed gentry, and two Catholics, one of whom was a land agent under police protection.

The crown was represented by a powerful legal team led by the attorney general, John Naish, Sergeant Robinson QC, The McDermot QC,[21] Francis Nolan QC and Mr F. le Poer Trench QC. The same counsel, Mr John Stritch QC and Mr Taylor QC, appeared for the defence. In opening the case for the crown, the attorney general asserted that Muldowney was identified running with Regan towards Rahasane House and that no fair-minded man could escape the conviction that the persons crossing the field were the persons who fired the shots. In fact, neither Moran nor Raftery identified anyone other than Regan in the field, either in their depositions or at the various trials.[22] The attorney general also referred to Muldowney's position as a constable and 'if the evidence satisfied the jury of his guilt, then the fact that he was a member of the constabulary was an awful aggravation of the offence with which he was charged'.[23] The attorney general further asserted that Regan was 'the leader in this outrage, the person who planned it, and a villain of the most awful and desperate type, who

<hr />

17 NAI CSO RP 1884/6369 and 6938 in 1888/13481.   18 Mathias McDonnell Bodkin QC, a native of Tuam, Co. Galway, was admitted to the bar in 1877. He was editor of *United Ireland* at the time of the 'Parnell split', and was elected MP for Roscommon north in 1892, defeating James J. O'Kelly. He was appointed county court judge for Clare in 1907. He was the author of several novels and historical works, including a biography of *Lord Edward Fitzgerald* (Dublin, n.d.) and *Famous Irish trials* (Dublin, 1918; 1997).   19 *Freeman's Journal*, 11 Mar. 1884.   20 *Tuam News*, 18 July 1884.   21 Hugh Hyacinth O'Rorke McDermot, AG 1892–5, and prince of Coolavin.   22 *Tuam News*, 18 July 1884.   23 Ibid.

had fled the country before the evidence was forthcoming'. The attorney general stated that Moran would prove the constitution of the shooting party and the disposition of the men at Doherty's house. However, the evidence given at the trials and in the depositions provided no corroboration for Moran's claims except that given by Raftery, who was not at the scene of the murder. The defence counsel referred to the disreputable character of Raftery, who was dismissed by two employers, Burton Persse and Isidore Bourke, because he had stolen sheep and potatoes. Raftery was closely questioned with regard to a number of discrepancies in his evidence such as:

a) the duration of his stay in Craughwell and the time of his departure from Craughwell – the defence lawyers suspected that the time was changed deliberately in order to conform more closely with Moran's story;

b) the fact that Mr Somerville, the engineer, had been given two versions of Raftery's position near the stile but he still concluded that Raftery would not have been able to see the stile from either position.[24]

During cross-examination by Mr Taylor, Raftery was asked: 'What made you give information first?' He replied: 'The police were always bothering me; it was Redington bothered me, he used to meet me on the road'. In relation to contacts with Moran, he was unable to say if he was speaking to Moran before he gave information. Kate Doherty referred to the dog following her brother into the stable and the fact that when the shooting occurred he jumped on the wall, barking furiously, whereas Moran, who claimed to be behind that wall, neither saw nor heard the dog. Kate also said that on the night of the killing she saw Muldowney sitting on the table in the kitchen. When she came into the kitchen, she said in a loud voice: 'Is Mr Muldowney there?' He made no answer and she did not see him go into the room where the body lay. It is difficult to provide an explanation for this episode because Kate Doherty should have known Muldowney, who had been engaged in patrols about their house during the boycott. However, it created an aura of suspicion and a sinister motivation was attributed to Muldowney's silence and failure to view the body. DI Alan Bell said that he discovered some ammunition in Regan's house, but this evidence was hardly surprising as Regan carried a gun for his own protection. As in the first trial, Margaret Raftery contradicted her husband's evidence, saying that he did not leave the house after nightfall.

An interesting account of Moran's cross-examination by Mr Taylor exposed several instances of perjury and an admission that he did not tell the truth in his first deposition:[25]

24 *Tuam News*, 18 July 1884. 25 *Sligo Champion*, 28 July 1884.

Taylor: Then you are a murderer and a perjurer.
Moran: I suppose so.
Taylor: You denied branding at first?
Moran: Well, one cannot always be exact.
Taylor: Did you ever say that you did not know who went with Regan?
Moran: I did know.
Taylor: Then the first statement was a perjury?
Moran: It was.
Taylor: That's another perjury, you swore here that you could not tell
         who you gave the gun to?
Moran: I was in such a bad way I did not know.
Taylor: What refreshed your memory?
Moran: I thought over it.

Moran's testimony does not seem credible, but the judge believed his story and also convinced the jury that his evidence deserved credence.

Several other discrepancies are evident in Moran's statements, particularly in his account of the arming of the group. In his first deposition he said that Regan gave everyone except Conway a gun; in his second deposition he said that Regan gave guns to Finnegan, Connolly and himself; and at the trial they all had guns except Conway. Similarly, Raftery's statements about the guns varied. In his first deposition, he said that only Regan had a gun; one week later, he claimed that Regan and Muldowney had guns and Fogarty something like a gun, and he repeated that at the trial. There was also conflict among the police officers regarding whether or not Muldowney carried a gun when he went to Craughwell. Constable Corcoran did not see one; Constable Judge said he had a double-barrelled gun and Muldowney did not think he had one. This also illustrates the problems of accurate recall of events that had taken place two-and-a-half years earlier.

Again, there was considerable controversy over the admissibility of several statements made by Muldowney when he was questioned before his arrest without being cautioned and was unaware that he was suspected of a crime (see above, p. 39). Counsel for the defence argued that Section 16 of the Prevention of Crime (Ireland) Act specifically disallowed use of such statements. Nevertheless, Judge Murphy allowed RM A.N. Brady to read the statement made on 3 February, which recounted Muldowney's visit to Craughwell and the return to Rahasane House. Brady alleged that Muldowney had stated:

On the day of the murder, Regan did not arrange with him to go to Craughwell together. They met on the way and Regan asked him to go with him. It was about half past 3 o'clock. He did not believe he had any rifle or gun with him and he had no revolver. He called at the barracks, and then bought some bacon and groceries. They drove back together as far as Aggard [Greenhouse] Cross and Regan told him to go round by the front gate as he wished to go and see some potatoes. He then ran down the road, and Regan's son and he [Muldowney] drove to the yard. It was not nightfall then. Constable Lee was in, and they both stopped in at supper chatting and reading the newspaper. He did not see Regan from the time he left him until he saw him at his [Regan's] own house.

It was claimed that Muldowney then said that

He remained at Regan's about an hour and was sitting at the fire when Constable Lee came in to tell of the murder. Regan said he would not stop by himself – that they would come and shoot him. Regan, on hearing of the murder, seemed greatly put out and he followed them to the big house. A fortnight after the murder Regan said 'Are the people saying anything about the murder' and he replied that the Dohertys were saying strange things. Regan then said 'They would hang me if they could'. He [Regan] was sick and seemed conscience stricken. He [Muldowney] never heard until he made the statement that he was suspected.

It was alleged that in another statement made on 4 February: 'Muldowney said he remembered saying that he was with Regan from 7 to 9 o'clock, but he now admitted he was not with him from dark until 9 o'clock. He could not explain why he did this'.[26] Omitted from the newspaper account but recorded in Judge Murphy's notes was another statement from Muldowney that corrected the time that he went to Regan's house to 8pm rather than 9pm, which would explain his absence from the policemen's room when Fox went there at about 8pm. The confused statements regarding the timing of his visit to Regan's house did not help Muldowney's case and it was suggested after the trial by RIC colleagues that Muldowney was afraid that he would be in breach of his guard duties if he was not in Regan's company all of that night and he therefore made the initial statement that cleared Regan of any involvement. CI Byrne of Galway East Riding, gave a character reference for Muldowney who had worked under his command for two years and he affirmed that Muldowney possessed the qualities necessary for protection duty, namely 'reliability of character, efficiency in the detection of crime and fidelity to duty'.[27] He also referred to him as 'specially zealous, faithful and trustworthy'. Mary Forde said that Muldowney came to Regan's house after nightfall and remained there until Constable Lee came to inform them of the murder. Unfortunately, previous statements made by Mary

26 *Tuam News*, 18 July 1884.   27 *Sligo Champion*, 28 July 1884.

Forde were contradictory and it was easy to set aside her alibi for Regan, which would otherwise have exposed the claims of Raftery and Moran. Addressing the jury for the defence, Mr Stritch QC spoke strongly about the 'outrageous probability of the story that a policeman of excellent character, without suggestion of motive, would participate in a brutal murder, or that a number of men, bent upon a deed of blood, would, without question or suspicion, accept a strange policeman in full uniform as an accomplice'.[28]

In the absence of a transcript of the trial evidence, the extensive notes recorded by Judge Murphy are a valuable record.[29] He noted the evidence of the two policemen who said that Regan and Muldowney were in Craughwell at about 2pm or 3pm and that they drove away in the direction of Cawley's between 5pm and 6pm. The judge did not acknowledge that these times were more consistent with Muldowney's version of events rather than the later timings of Raftery and Moran. The judge placed great emphasis on a statement by Muldowney (not included in newspaper accounts) that referred to his sighting of a group of men at Aggard Bridge on his way back with Regan to Rahasane House. Among the group he recognized Finnegan, Fogarty and Conway and Judge Murphy commented: 'How could Moran have known, if inventing a story, that five of the men he was falsely accusing would be known to have met at this bridge on the evening of 2 November?' Collusion between Raftery and Moran in the fabrication of evidence was strongly suspected by the defence counsel and it is quite possible that Raftery, on his way home to Rahasane, was indeed passed by Regan and Muldowney on the side-car and also encountered the other men on the road. Finnegan at that time was working for John W. Lambert at Aggard House and would have walked the short distance to his home, which was on the same road. It is also possible that Fogarty and Conway were working in the area and their presence on the road was of an entirely innocent nature. It would have been a simple matter to delay the time of the meeting of Raftery and the men to later that evening in order to coincide with Moran's version.

In his charge to the jury, Judge Murphy stated that 'Raftery was not an approver and if his evidence was believed the prisoner was guilty'. Moran, he said,

> was clearly an accomplice and though they would be at liberty to find a verdict of guilty on his evidence alone, if it brought home conviction to their minds, still I should advise them not to act on his evidence unless they found independent evidence that led them to believe he was not inventing the whole story.

Murphy went on to outline what he considered to be independent evidence if Raftery's evidence was excluded from the case [comments in square brackets are arguments put forward by the present author]:

28 *Galway Vindicator*, 16 July 1884. **29** NAI CSO RP Misc. 03/396.

a) The numbers in the two parties, one opposite and one at the side of the house. [In fact none of the Dohertys referred to the numbers in the groups at this trial. In Finnegan's second trial, Kate Doherty referred to only three men going away (see below, p. 67).

b) The two volleys of shots that were heard. [This was confirmed by the Dohertys and by the forensic evidence.]

c) The mode in which the groups made off. [Kate Doherty said that one group ran down the boreen in the opposite direction to the house and another group went around to the left by the barn. Moran made no reference to the first group.]

d) John Doherty's identification of Regan's voice. [Doherty said: 'While I was running I heard a voice saying that "there was someone coming" or "someone down", I don't know which. It fitted in my heart that the voice was Regan's'. Under cross-examination, he said he could not swear to it.]

e) The fact of the Dohertys' suspicions of Regan's involvement on the night of the murder. [Apart from John Doherty's belief that he heard Regan's voice there was no visual identification of Regan by the Dohertys. They knew Regan well and already believed that Regan had organized the boycott.]

f) The reply of the prisoner to Mary Anne Doherty that he was with Regan all the evening. [This was interpreted as placing both men at the murder scene rather than acceptance of Muldowney's claim that he was in Rahasane House and later in Regan's house all of that night. Although given in evidence at the trial, it was not included in Mary Anne's original deposition.][30]

g) Muldowney's statement to DI Bell, when Bell was making enquiries about Regan, that he was in Regan's company between 7pm and 10pm. [It was unfortunate for Muldowney that he linked himself with Regan because that (in the view of the judge, the police and the investigating magistrates) also placed him at the murder scene.]

h) That Muldowney and Regan met Finnegan, Fogarty and Conway at Aggard Bridge on their way back to Rahasane House. [An alternative explanation was that the men were all natives of the area and the meeting was a casual one and, in any case, the encounter would have occurred much earlier than the one described by Raftery.]

i) The statement of James Fox that Muldowney was not in Rahasane House at 8pm was interpreted as indicating that he was absent with Regan and at the murder scene. [Muldowney's contradictory state-

---

30 Judge's notes: 'I saw prisoner coming in. He sat on corner of table. I came to him and said Mr Muldowney when did you see Regan. He said he was in Regan's company all the evening till the murder was reported'.

ments regarding the time of his departure for Regan's house certainly did not help his case.]

j) The statements of Constable Corcoran and Sergeant Judge placing Regan and Muldowney in Craughwell on that day. [This was at a much earlier time than Moran claimed. The fact that they were driving towards Cawley's public house was explained by the fact that it was on their way home and did not imply that they stopped there. In addition, the police evidence referred to them passing Cawley's but not stopping there.]

The contradictions in Moran's two depositions as well as in the evidence given at the trial were not alluded to in Judge Murphy's notes or in the newspaper accounts. Judge Murphy dismissed the evidence given by two defence witnesses, Margaret Raftery and John Healy. These witnesses placed Raftery in his house at Rahasane all the evening and night and placed Moran drunk and staggering along the road several miles away on the other side of Craughwell. Nevertheless, Judge Murphy concluded that each gave a narrative of what occurred on the night of 2 November, one account in January 1883 and the other three months later, that was in several particulars proved to be correct by independent evidence. Judge Murphy accepted the evidence of the two informers and set aside the contrary evidence of the defence witnesses that Raftery and Moran were elsewhere at the time of the murder. It is argued in the discussion of Murphy's document (above) that no credible corroboration was provided by independent evidence. In fact, Margaret Raftery became so distressed by her husband's role as an informer and his responsibility for the arrest of innocent people that she refused to have anything more to do with him. Judge Murphy may have regarded her as a tainted witness, because he noted that she had visited Finnegan on two occasions when she was in Sligo for the assizes and brought clothes to him from his mother.

Judge Murphy did not comment on Moran's evidence that no one other than Peter Doherty came out of the house even though Kate Doherty stated that she accompanied her brother. There is no reference in the notes to the barking of the dog as stated by Kate Doherty and that the dog jumped onto the wall behind which Moran claimed to have been. Moran said he did not see the dog or hear it barking.

There was no reference in the judge's notes to the forensic evidence from the post mortem examination by Dr Leonard and no analysis of the significance of the trajectory of the fatal bullet. The evidence clearly contradicted Moran's claim that the first shots came from the haggard and that Doherty fell. If this claim were true, the bullet would have struck Doherty in the back and not in the left shoulder. This should have raised serious doubts about the validity of Moran's statement.

In conclusion, Judge Murphy stated that the evidence of Raftery and Moran was corroborated by independent evidence and according to the *Sligo Champion* he charged the jury in terms unfavourable to the prisoner. Murphy's interpretation of the evidence must have had a significant effect on the deliberations of the jury because, just over two hours later, they found Muldowney guilty and the judge sentenced him to be hanged in Galway Jail on 12 August 1884. After the verdict, Muldowney said: 'I am convicted of a murder I know nothing about, no more than the child unborn. Commit murder indeed, with Jack Moran'.[31] In relation to the dispatch of policemen to request Constable Lee's return from America to give evidence, Muldowney said that he had received a statement from a man in America who claimed that he was not asked to return to give evidence but to swear that he did not see Muldowney at Rahasane House on the evening of the murder.

Judge Murphy stated that 'the evidence was in my opinion clear and conclusive'. When Lord Spencer was deciding whether or not to commute the death sentence, he underlined this damning sentence with his characteristic blue pencil. It was to appear again and again in response to the numerous petitions lodged subsequently for the release of the prisoners.

The jury members signed a statement unanimously recommending Muldowney to mercy. The grounds stated were:

1 Muldowney was drawn into the commission of this crime through the influence of James Regan whom he was protecting and with whom he was constantly associated in the discharge of his official duty;
2 His youth made him susceptible to the evil influence of Regan, who led him astray, and as he received an excellent character from his CI Byrne, the jury trust that your lordship will take the most merciful view of his case.

The signatures included James Nelson, foreman, John Pettegrew, Simon Cullen, James Powell, Henry Brett, Thadeus Conboy, Robert Shaw, Robert Warren, Thomas Dorran, John White, Edward Martin and Robert Porteus. Judge Murphy said that, unless Muldowney belonged to a secret society before he joined the force, it was almost certain that it was Regan who corrupted him. This remark raises the possibility that Judge Murphy may have been aware of claims made by another informer, James Gavin, that Muldowney was a member of a secret society (see below, p. 89). The attorney general, however, refused to admit Gavin's statement in evidence. If the judge knew about these claims during the trial, it could have biased his judgment against the prisoner.

A press report of the trial[32] commented that 'at every street corner, the cry

31 *Tuam News*, 1 Aug. 1884. 32 Ibid.

was – no one expected he would be found guilty'. One remark was 'Oh rotten Sligo, it can give a jury to do any work'. DI Lawless reported to CI Ross that a stranger had made threatening remarks to one of the jurors, James Powell, in the hearing of his brother. The stranger was Dr Dalton, who had performed the post mortem examination on Peter Doherty and had given evidence in the trial. He was alleged to have said 'that no jury in Ireland could find such a verdict' and when a remark was made that there were three Catholics on the jury Dalton responded 'they were no Catholics for they were under police protection'.[33] Some of the jurors were attacked entering the Imperial Hotel and another, Simon Cullen, was hissed at while passing through the town. There was criticism of the one-sided nature of the judge's charge to the jury and it was claimed that he behaved more like a crown prosecutor than a judge, participating at length in the cross-examination of witnesses. Any discrepancy in the evidence of Moran and Raftery was described as 'very trifling, scarcely worthy of the jury's attention' and, significantly, he did not comment on the disreputable characters of Moran and Raftery.

33 NAI CSO RP, 1884/17518, Lawless to Ross, 22 July 1884.

5 The trials of Patrick Finnegan

THE FIRST TRIAL, SLIGO SUMMER ASSIZES, JULY 1884

The first trial of Finnegan commenced at Sligo assizes on 23 July 1884 before Judge Murphy. The account in the *Tuam News* described Finnegan as 'a comfortably dressed young man of the farming class'. When called upon to plead, he said 'I am as innocent of that as you are, sir, if I get justice'.[1] The defence counsels were George Orme Malley[2] and Mathias McDonnell Bodkin and on this occasion the jury was composed entirely of Protestants. The attorney general presented the case for the crown and stated that it would be proved that Finnegan was one of those concealed behind the wall at the Dohertys' house and that he fired at Peter Doherty Junior. Again, Regan was vilified: 'the leader in this business was the steward, Regan – a man of villainous and bad character who leagued himself with some of those dreadful secret societies that existed in that part of the country'.[3] The attorney general's understanding of the case can be gauged from his assertion that the gang was brought to Doherty's house by Raftery 'who had no part in the business'.[4] It is remarkable that someone who was present for the entire proceedings of Muldowney's trial a week earlier could have made such a statement, having heard Raftery say that he had walked along the road to Rahasane without any mention of going to Peter Doherty's house. The attorney general also referred to the lack of patrols at Doherty's house on the night of the murder because of the extra policemen guarding the 'Emergency Men' at Aggard House, which allowed the 'band of assassins to meet without hindrance'.[5] He did not seem to appreciate that the extra police were placed very close to Aggard Bridge, the alleged meeting place of the shooting party according to the evidence of Raftery and Moran (fig. 4, p. 41).

The evidence presented was broadly similar to that given during the second trial of Muldowney. Mr Taylor for the defence again questioned Raftery about possible collusion with Moran regarding their evidence. When asked about any conversation with Moran between the time of the murder and making his deposition, he said categorically: 'Indeed I had not'. He claimed that they were not even on speaking terms. Yet, in the trial of Muldowney during the previous week, Raftery was unable to say or swear if he was talking to Moran before he gave information. The remarkable improvement of his memory suggests tuition from DI Bell and Sergeant Redington in the interval between the two trials.

Moran, on this occasion, was unable to say where Finnegan was placed at the murder scene, whereas in all previous evidence he placed him in the same group

---

1 *Tuam News*, 25 July 1884. 2 George Orme Malley, admitted to the bar in 1843, QC 1868. 3 *Tuam News*, 25 July 1884. 4 Ibid. 5 Ibid.

as himself, at the wall in front of the house. He again referred to the first volley of shots coming from the haggard and Doherty falling as a result. The second volley then came from in front of the house. In none of the newspaper accounts of the trials or in Judge Murphy's notes was there any analysis of this statement. The forensic evidence of the trajectory of the bullet from the left shoulder through the body to exit at the right shoulder clearly indicates that the fatal shot came from the wall in front of the house and this was the position that Moran allegedly occupied. Moran was later recalled at the request of a juror who asked about the murder scene. Moran said that no one came out of the house except Peter Doherty. This is in direct conflict with the consistent evidence of Kate Doherty, who said she came out of the house with her brother. Moran's failure to see or hear the dog was again confirmed. However, Judge Murphy, in his charge to the jury, attached little importance to the discrepancies between Moran's account and the account of Kate Doherty, who was undoubtedly at the scene.[6]

During the second Muldowney trial, Kate Doherty said that while she was leaning over the body of her brother she saw a man looking over the wall at her. She believed it was Finnegan. Under cross-examination she said that she did not mention anything about Finnegan when she was first examined and did not do so until after the prisoners were arrested, but she claimed that she had mentioned the name of Finnegan to her parents and to SI Bell and County Inspector Byrne before that. Now, in Finnegan's trial, she said that a man looked at her over the wall opposite the door. 'She could not say who he was, but it struck her that it was Finnegan, whom she had known before'.[7] It is worth recalling what she said in her deposition of 3 March 1883:

> I saw the figure of a man standing at the other side of the yard wall. The man saw me and made off as fast as if I was going to shoot him. I had not sufficient time to identify the man; he got away too quickly, and I had not a dry eye at the time. Judging from the view I got of the man, I believed the man I saw there at the wall was Finnegan.[8]

Kate gave another version of her evidence at the compensation hearings held in November 1882. On that occasion, she said that she saw 'the shadows of some men but did not see their persons'.[9] It is surely extraordinary that such a vague identification was accepted as sworn testimony in the deposition and as valid evidence during the trials to establish Finnegan's presence at the murder scene. This vague description was also accepted as a corroboration of Moran's claims.

A man called William Geoghegan said he lived close to Raftery's house and

6 *Tuam News*, 1 Aug. 1884.   7 *Tuam News*, 25 July 1884.   8 NAI CRF misc. 1903/484, Crown brief for the solicitor general.   9 *Galway Vindicator*, 2 Dec. 1882.

he recounted a conversation he had with him during which, he claimed, Raftery said: 'Muldowney and Regan had gone to America and those that would swear something against them would be well paid by the crown'.[10] In reply, Geoghegan said: 'What could I swear against them? I know nothing about them'. Then Raftery said: 'Whisht you fool. You don't know how to live at all'. Patrick Loughrey swore that Finnegan was with him in Cawley's pub until 8.30pm. A statement made by him to Bell and Redington was produced which stated that the time was 7pm. Loughrey said he did not mention the hour in the statement, which would suggest that the time was added as a deliberate attempt on Bell's part to deprive Finnegan of an alibi. Michael Skehill swore that he saw Finnegan and Loughrey in Cawley's but did not see Joyce, Fogarty, Connolly, Muldowney or any of the others there that night.

Mr Malley opened the case for the defence and said

> his defence was that this was not a case of mistaken identity, but non-identity. It would be proved that the previous career of the prisoner had been unimpeachable, that he bore the highest possible character and that no particle of suspicion could be laid against him. There was not a word of evidence from beginning to end to show that Finnegan was influenced by unworthy or malicious motives towards the Dohertys.[11]

Malley went on to say: 'that wretched creature John Moran was put forward to strengthen Raftery's evidence and with the hardihood that characterized the trained informer he answered that he was proud of his character but a blacker or more infamous character was never disclosed in a court of justice'.[12] He also commented that Kate Doherty's identification of the prisoner 'was of the loosest character' and her evidence that the members of the shooting party departed in two different directions was also inconsistent with Moran's evidence that all the participants ran away at once. Sergeant Robinson QC concluded the case for the crown with the quite untrue statement that 'Moran's evidence was corroborated in all its essential features by the independent testimony and that the case for the crown was complete in every detail – there was no missing link or weak point in the chain of evidence'.[13]

Judge Murphy's address to the jury began with a moralizing lecture on their duties and his own responsibilities. He strongly defended Raftery's evidence and his failure to bring it to the attention of the police at an earlier stage on the grounds that if he gave information to the police he would have been ostracized in the local community. In a convoluted argument, the judge suggested that the reason Raftery did not attempt to implicate the Morrisseys when they were arrested soon after the murder was that 'he would not venture to get up a totally

10 *Tuam News*, 25 July 1884.   11 Ibid.   12 Ibid.   13 Ibid.

false statement'. If the judge gave a balanced account of the case for the defence, it is not contained in the newspaper accounts that referred to him glossing over the imperfect identification of Finnegan at the murder scene and he failed to mention the evidence that both Moran and Raftery were elsewhere at the time of the crime.

The jury retired at midday and returned at 1.45pm, when the foreman said the jury had given the case the best possible consideration and they could not arrive at a conclusion. The judge said 'he would not feel warranted in discharging them at present. It was a case of great importance, and they must give it more consideration'. At 4.15pm the jury returned and the foreman announced that 'there was not the slightest chance of their agreeing to a verdict'. The case was adjourned to 5 August and the judge said that the special jurors would be expected to attend or pay fines of £100. In a letter to the county inspector, DI Alan Bell said it was no surprise that the jury disagreed 'because there were only seven good jurors on the panel'.[14]

According to the correspondent of the *Tuam News*, Finnegan's calm demeanour and manly bearing in the dock won for him the admiration and sympathy of all who saw him except those who thirsted for his blood. On his way to the courthouse he said to friends 'if it is God's will that I must be hanged on the lying testimony of Patsy Raftery and the ruffian Moran, I am ready for it – prepared to die'.[15]

SIGNIFICANT DEVELOPMENTS BEHIND THE SCENES

Legal bargaining
Before the next trial, there were several important developments. First, it became known that the prisoners' counsel had made a very strong appeal to them to plead guilty.[16] Another report indicated that the crown solicitor had offered to withdraw the charge of murder if the prisoners would plead guilty to a charge of conspiracy to murder and a sentence of ten years penal servitude would then be imposed.[17] In the House of Commons, Tim Healy MP asked the Solicitor General if the crown had made an offer to withdraw the capital charge if the prisoners would consent to plead guilty to a charge of conspiracy. In typically convoluted language, the reply stated that

> the advisors of the prisoners applied to the crown to know if a plea on a minor charge would be accepted. This plea was not accepted, but the advisors of the prisoners were afterwards informed that such a plea would be considered, if received, but no undertaking could be given.[18]

14 NAI CSO RP 1885/5161, DI Bell to CI Byrne, 1 Aug. 1884. 15 *Tuam News*, 1 Aug. 1884.
16 Ibid. 17 *Connaught People*, 2 Aug. 1884. 18 *Freeman's Journal*, 9 Aug. 1884.

The prisoners indignantly refused to plead guilty, however, and reaffirmed their innocence of the crime they were alleged to have committed. The father of Michael Fogarty was interviewed and he said: 'I would sooner my son would die a thousand deaths on the scaffold than plead guilty, because he and all the poor fellows are innocent'.[19] The prisoners also rejected a second request from their solicitor a few days later. Another shock for Finnegan was the decision by George Orme Malley, who was a defence counsel in the first trial, to withdraw from the case at very short notice.[20]

The Prisoners' Defence Fund and Fair Trial Fund
Under the provisions of the Prevention of Crime (Ireland) Act of 1882, the expenses of the defence counsel and witnesses were paid by the government but it was widely believed that defence counsel assigned to the accused were of inferior quality compared to the powerful legal teams who prosecuted. This belief led to the collection of funds for the purpose of employing independent counsel. Soon after the prisoners' arrest in 1883, an anonymous letter appeared in the *Western News* urging the inauguration of a fund for the prisoners' defence and support.[21] A further report confirmed the establishment of such a fund[22] and Edward Barrett from Craughwell left for America at the end of April to solicit contributions for the fund.[23]

After the conviction of Muldowney, there must have been dissatisfaction with the performance of the defence counsel because another fund was launched. It was called the Fair Trial Fund and its purpose was to obtain the 'best legal ability in Ireland to defend the accused … and secure them as fair a trial as can be had under English law in Ireland.'[24] The announcement was signed by Poor Law Guardian Patrick Cawley, Michael Carr, Michael Cloonan and John Dolan and it referred to the fact that there was not a single Catholic on the jury for Finnegan's first trial. The committee received sufficient contributions to secure the services of Dr T.E. Webb QC, Regius Professor of Law at Trinity College, for the second trial.[25] By the end of August, a sum of £261 had been collected at church gate collections in Craughwell, Loughrea, Gort and Athenry and from personal contributions. The published list of subscribers to the fund included £10 from a 'defender of innocence and a hater of official scoundrellism'. A sum of £20 came from 'one who is horrified with the ruffianly conduct of government officials'.[26]

19 *Connaught People*, 2 Aug. 1884. 20 *Tuam News*, 8 Aug. 1884. 21 *Western News*, 24 Feb. 1883. 22 *Western News*, 17 Mar. 1883. 23 *Western News*, 5 May 1883. 24 *Tuam News*, 18 July 1884. 25 Thomas Ebenezer Webb (1821–1903), MA, LLB, LLD, TCD in 1859. Professor of moral philosophy, Dublin University, 1857–67; regius professor of laws at TCD, 1867–87. Regarded as a talented barrister and remembered for a brilliant cross-examination of the informers in connection with the Phoenix Park murders. He became county court judge for Donegal in 1888. Author of a verse translation of Goethe's *Faust*, the *Mystery of William Shakespeare* and a pamphlet on the Irish land question. 26 *Tuam News*, 29 Aug. 1884.

SECOND TRIAL OF PATRICK FINNEGAN,
SLIGO SUMMER ASSIZES, AUGUST 1884

The second trial of Finnegan began on 5 August and the fact that Judge James Murphy again presided did not augur well for the accused. The attorney general, John Naish, Sergeant Robinson QC, Mr Nolan QC and Mr le Poer Trench QC represented the crown. As well as Special Counsel Dr Webb, McDonnell Bodkin QC defended. Controversy arose immediately regarding the composition of the jury. When the names of jurors who had served in the first trial were called, they indicated that they had their minds made up about the case and they expressed the wish to be excused. The crown did not agree and said the jurors should be sworn in. Mr Francis McCormick, for the defence, challenged those jurors and they were excluded, but when he had exhausted his quota of challenges, Robert Porteous, who had served on the jury that convicted Muldowney, was called. Porteous said: 'My Lord, I don't wish to serve on the jury. I don't think it is right I should be asked to serve, as I have my mind made up already. It is not at all fair to the prisoner that I should serve on the jury'.[27] Presumably, he had decided that Finnegan was guilty. The attorney general rejected his plea and insisted that he serve and with supreme irony he went on to advise the jury to approach this case as if they had never heard of it until they were sworn in. It will be seen in ch. 7 that individuals served on multiple juries trying prisoners charged with the same offence.

When the attorney general introduced the case for the crown, he claimed with characteristic inaccuracy that all the men carried guns and that Raftery saw the party pass by Doherty's house. During the trial, much of the evidence was repeated with minor variations. An important admission came from Moran when he agreed with Dr Webb that he had committed perjury on two occasions. The press report referred to Moran writhing and trembling in the witness box and saying several times that he did not understand Dr Webb's questions.[28] In relation to the identification of Finnegan at the scene, Kate Doherty said she saw the shadows of three men going away; she believed one was the shadow of a man – portion of his body was over the wall; she thought it was the shadow of Finnegan, 'but she was not sure'. Sergeant Redington said he went over the ground with the engineer who concluded that the stile could not be seen from the position indicated. The following day, Raftery indicated a different position, but the engineer claimed that the view was much the same from both positions. Redington made an important admission when he said that he had many conversations with Raftery and he had sent many reports to his officers, but the notebook with the original entries had been destroyed and therefore could not be produced in court. These reports may have been included in a file[29] given to DI

27 *Tuam News*, 12 Sept. 1884. 28 *Tuam News*, 15 Aug. 1884. 29 NAI CSO RP 1884/6005, 3 Mar. 1884.

Bell immediately before the first trial of Muldowney, but are no longer present among the documents in the National Archives of Ireland. According to the CSO register for 1884, this file contained original information regarding the police investigations of the case. The last record in the CSO register shows that the file was signed out to DI Alan Bell on the eve of Muldowney's first trial and it is perhaps not surprising that Bell would have wished to conceal confidential information.

Dr Webb addressed the jury for one-and-a-half hours and referred to the manly, honest countenance of the prisoner, compared with the 'hang dog look of the two scoundrels who are trying to swear his life away. Society would not be safe if such scoundrels' oaths could be relied on'. He stated that the defence case was that 'Raftery and Moran concocted the story' and that their testimony was a case of one scoundrel corroborating another. Webb said he was amused by the attempt made by the crown to prove that Raftery and Moran had no communication with one another, whereas 'out of his own mouth, and he believed it was the only piece of truth he told, Raftery said that he met Moran and spoke to him, had many conversations with him'.[30] Webb also ridiculed Raftery's inability to recognize Moran, whom he had known since childhood and he strongly denounced the prosecution for altering the map of the alleged route to try to suit Raftery's statement. Webb described the identification of Finnegan at the scene as worthless and for the first time in the trials he analyzed the forensic details to reject Moran's claim that the fatal bullet was fired from the haggard. He claimed that Moran committed perjury because of the contradictory statements in his depositions and the evidence he gave in court.

Sergeant Robinson, QC for the crown, tried to undermine Margaret Raftery's evidence by saying that Raftery did go out on the evening of the murder and that he saw Regan and Muldowney on the car. In support of this contention, Robinson referred to the statement of James Fox that he met Raftery, but in fact this meeting took place much earlier in the afternoon before Raftery and the others left Rahasane to go to Craughwell. Nevertheless, Robinson claimed that the evidence of Fox destroyed the whole evidence of Margaret Raftery. He acknowledged that 'Moran's character was bad enough' and that his evidence required corroboration, but he argued that Raftery had provided such.

In his charge to the jury, Judge Murphy said that it was 'part of his duty to strive that true and reliable evidence should not be put aside' and suggested that if the jury believed that neither Moran nor Raftery was inventing the story, then the guilt of the prisoner was established. He went on to state that 'judges were accustomed to advise jurors not to act on the evidence of a man like Moran unless there was independent corroborating evidence'. Murphy argued that Moran's evidence had been partly corroborated by the Dohertys, but in fact it

30 *Tuam News*, 15 Aug. 1884.

had differed on several crucial points. For example, Moran said that only Peter Doherty came out of the house, he did not see the dog or hear it barking, and he gave a different account of the manner in which the groups had departed the murder scene. The judge concluded by saying that if there was a doubt that either Moran or Raftery was at the scene of the murder they should acquit the prisoner, but he did not comment on the clear evidence of Margaret Raftery and John Healy that placed them elsewhere.

The jury retired at 4.50pm and returned at 6.25pm with the verdict that the prisoner was guilty of conspiracy to murder. Judge Murphy responded that they could not find that verdict; if the prisoner conspired to murder Doherty he was guilty of murder in the eyes of the law. Dr Webb argued that the reverse was laid down as law during the Phoenix Park murder cases, but the judge did not accept this argument. The jury returned a second time and the foreman said that some of the jurors were not satisfied with the identification of Finnegan in the party that left Aggard Bridge for Doherty's house. However, the judge said that 'the prisoner was identified at the bridge by Raftery as well as Moran. Finally, at 6.50pm, the jury returned a verdict of guilty of murder but the foreman stated that the jury had unanimously agreed to recommend the prisoner to mercy.

When called upon, Finnegan stood forward in the dock and vehemently declared his innocence. He said 'he was no more guilty than the foreman of the jury' and, thumping the front rail of the dock, he said he never murdered or conspired to murder anyone. He said that he forgave Raftery and Moran, who would do anything for whiskey. He referred to his presence in Cawley's public house on the night of the murder, saying he did not see Muldowney, Regan or any of the other prisoners that night. He also said that Muldowney had been condemned, but he knew nothing about the murder. Judge Murphy told Finnegan that he was found guilty on the most conclusive evidence by a jury who were extremely anxious to find a verdict in his favour if they possibly could. This was an ironical comment in view of the fact that one member, Robert Porteous, had declared that his mind was made up before the trial began. The judge said that he believed that 'prior to this event, the prisoner led a blameless life, being employed in the neighbourhood as a shepherd, but, having been drawn into this terrible conspiracy, he became bound hand and foot by wretched men who dragged him into trouble'. Finnegan interjected that he never conspired: 'I never took part in it, nor was I there; I had no knowledge of it no more than the child unborn' and concluded by saying that he did not see Peter Doherty on the night of the shooting. Judge Murphy donned the black cap and sentenced him to be hanged in Galway Jail on 27 August 1884.[31]

The verdict was greeted with dismay and anger in Galway and Sligo, with much condemnatory comment in the press, particularly in the *Tuam News* and

31 *Tuam News*, 8 Aug. 1884; 15 Aug. 1884.

Sligo Champion. There was widespread unease about the selection of the jury, especially the inclusion of Robert Porteous and the fact that all the members of the jury were Protestant. The role of Moran and Raftery in the trials was severely criticized, particularly that of Moran, who had taken several false oaths and made several false statements in connection with his evidence. There was reference to the strong belief that Sergeant Redington had concocted the entire story and that the defence witnesses had never made the statements he had attributed to them. The Loughrea correspondent expressed the fear that the conduct of the crown 'will inflame the people's passions, and incite them to commit desperate deeds'. Finnegan was removed from Sligo Jail on 8 August and was able to speak to the large number of people who gathered on the railway platform. He said that when the crown learned he would not plead guilty to conspiracy to murder, he was offered a free pardon and a lot of money if he would swear away the lives of his innocent comrades. He also spoke to Jack Moran, who was returning to the crown witness depot in Dublin: 'Ah Jack, Jack, you and Raftery have sworn my life away for money and whiskey. May the Lord forgive ye. Every word you and Raftery swore was false'.[32]

AN ALTERNATIVE NARRATIVE

If the testimony of Raftery and Moran was indeed false, is there an alternative narrative? Family members of Patrick Finnegan conducted the background research for this book over many years, extending back to the period when there were individuals alive with clear recollections of the events of that period. There was a consistency in the accounts about the participants in the Doherty and Bourke killings, although clearly these claims are unverifiable. The local version alleged that the shooting party consisted of men from Roveagh and Killeeneen, Brian Grealish, Brian Melvin and Patch Garvey and the man who released the horse from the stable was Dominic Keane from Carrigan. It is believed that the Morrisseys took part in organizing the shooting and that they purchased whiskey in Cawleys for those in the shooting party. The involvement of personnel from Roveagh is of interest because it was the Roveagh branch of the Land League that condemned the actions of the Dohertys when they took the disputed land in 1880 and it subsequently organized the boycott of the Dohertys.

The route taken by the shooting party to the murder scene was probably quite different to that described by Raftery and Moran. On the night of the killing, there was a large force of police guarding the 'Emergency Men' working at Lambert's estate at Aggard, and a body of armed men approaching from the

32 *Tuam News*, 12 Sept. 1884.

Craughwell direction would, therefore, have been in danger of detection and arrest. As information would have been readily available regarding police movements in the locality, the more likely approach route would have been around the south-western end of the Rahasane turlough at Rinn.

After the killing of Peter Doherty, it is believed that they took a more direct route to John Doherty's house than the more difficult route described by the informers. And after the shooting at John Doherty's, they could have retraced their steps to Rinn at the south-western end of Rahasane turlough and would not have passed Aggard House, where the 'Emergency Men' and their police guard were located.

Therefore, two men who were widely acknowledged to be innocent of the crime were condemned to death on fabricated evidence and perjured testimony. Finnegan's involvement in the Land League could conceivably have identified him as a suspect, but the sheer absurdity of Muldowney's conviction is astounding. He was a man who came from a loyal background and had an unblemished record of service in the RIC and enjoyed strong support from his fellow policemen. This record did not benefit him during his years of incarceration and indeed, as we will see, he was the victim of deliberate vindictiveness by the authorities.

Because of the disturbed nature of the area and the number of unsolved murders, the authorities feared the development of a lawless society controlled by secret societies and the Fenians. There was a great desire to impose the rule of law and neither effort nor money was spared to achieve this aim. The two members of the police force who led the investigations and who were believed to have fabricated the evidence were both rewarded for their achievements. Alan Bell was promoted to DI and later to a post as RM. Constable Redington became a sergeant and later a Head Constable. As we will see in ch. 6, the informers were well rewarded for their part in the perversion of justice.

6 The aftermath of the trials

Michael Muldowney was convicted and sentenced to death on 16 July 1884 and on the following day a letter was sent from Galway to Prime Minister Gladstone. It stated that 'in the opinion of every intelligent [person] here, ex-Constable Muldowney is innocent of the terrible crime'. There was reference to the bad conduct of the witnesses Moran and Raftery and the writer expressed surprise that 'the crown for a moment would believe that a policeman would associate with such persons or be guilty of such an awful crime'. The letter was signed by 'A lover of justice'. A handwriting expert (name now unknown) identified the writer as Daniel McDonagh, whose father had been a member of the RIC. Another letter was addressed to Queen Victoria, affirming Muldowney's innocence and referring to the disgraceful character of the informers. The police suspected that a young woman called Crawford, who had been present at the trial and was related to Muldowney, wrote the letter.[1] On 24 July, a memorial prepared by fourteen members of the RIC was sent to Dublin Castle. It strongly asserted the unanimous belief of members of the RIC that Muldowney was innocent of the crime. Reference was made to the evidence of 'two wretched men, Moran and Raftery, which could not be relied on for a moment'. The memorial claimed that Muldowney, when stating that he was with Regan on the night of the murder, intended to convey to his superior officers that he was fulfilling his duty to protect Regan. They laid emphasis on the manner that SRM Clifford Lloyd, RM A.N. Brady and DI John D. Phillips obtained Muldowney's earlier statements without informing him that he was suspected of a crime. The memorial further claimed that the investigating officers composed the document in such a manner as to support the informers' version of events and that as a result many of Muldowney's remarks were omitted. It concluded with an impassioned plea to grant 'mercy to a man whom we believe has been unjustly condemned'.[2] CI Byrne reported to Colonel Robert Bruce, inspector general of the RIC, that he did not believe 'that the memorial emanated from the police force, although I have no doubt but some of those who were in Sligo formed a belief in Muldowney's innocence'.[3] In a marginal note, the inspector general commented 'I am aware that the county inspector of Galway West Riding considers that a strong feeling in favour of Muldowney exists among the force there and in the force generally'. In a further communication to the inspector general on 4 August, Byrne, having made enquiries in

1 NAI CRF misc. 1903/484. 2 Ibid. 3 Ibid.

72

Sligo and Galway, stated that he was 'convinced the police had no part in getting up or forwarding the memorial'. He went on to state that 'the feeling amongst the force generally and in both districts of Galway is one of great sympathy for Muldowney as they believe he is not guilty of the murder'. Byrne also referred to several conversations he had with HC Wynne, who 'always asserted that Muldowney is innocent of the murder but guilty of concealing the perpetrators'. Wynne claimed that he had a better opportunity of forming an opinion as he had several interviews with the prisoners. At his last interview, 'Muldowney talked of his execution as calmly as if it were a matter of ordinary routine life and that he was quite resigned to his fate for he had no doubt of his salvation as he was going to the scaffold an innocent man'.[4]

Simon Cullen, justice of the peace of Thornhill House, Sligo, who had acted on the jury, sent a petition signed by all jury members to the lord lieutenant pleading for mercy for Muldowney. He revealed that 'one of the jurors after two hours refused to agree to a verdict of guilty'. After the jury retired a second time, the same juror 'still dissented against a verdict which would be followed by a sentence of death'. He only agreed to the verdict on the understanding that the death sentence would inevitably be commuted. A further memorial followed from Lady Frances Mary Granard, pleading for commutation of the death sentence and she enclosed a letter from Revd J. Corcoran, chaplain to Sligo Jail, urging clemency.[5] Richard Jennings, solicitor for the defence, forwarded two petitions requesting clemency to Lord Spencer, the first of which bore 210 signatures of citizens of Galway city and county, including Dr Carr, bishop of Galway and Kilmacduagh, eighteen other clergymen, James Morris MP, Sir Valentine Blake, five justices of the peace and numerous public representatives. It referred to the first trial of Muldowney at the spring assizes, which 'after two days ended in disagreement, when we are credibly informed and believe, one juror only was satisfied of the prisoner's guilt' and the fact that the jury also found it difficult to reach agreement in the second trial. In a comment on his seven years in the police force, the petition recalled CI Byrne's excellent character reference for Michael Muldowney 'which we have been assured and believe can be corroborated by many members of the force to which he belonged'. The second petition, from Sligo Corporation, was proposed by Councillor James Nelson, foreman of the jury that convicted him, and signed by Bernard Colleary, mayor of Sligo. This outpouring of sympathy for Muldowney leaves no doubt about the widespread public opinion regarding his innocence of the murder.

The question of commutation of the sentence of death received the closest attention from Lord Spencer, who asked the opinion of the lord chancellor, Edward Sullivan.[6] The reply on 4 August advised that 'the recommendation of

---

4 NAI CRF misc. 1903/484.   5 Ibid. 1903/396.   6 Edward Sullivan (1822–85), called to the bar 1848, QC 1858, MP and solicitor general 1865, attorney general 1868, created baronet 1881,

the jury can be safely acted on by not having the capital sentence carried out'. Lord Spencer had returned to his residence, Althorp, on 7 August and communicated with the under secretary, Sir Robert Hamilton, by telegram in cipher. He advised that the lord chancellor and Judge Murphy be asked if the conviction of Finnegan had any material affect on the decision regarding Muldowney. 'I am disposed to commute Muldowney, but think that the two should be treated together. I would go over tomorrow if there is the least ground for discussion'. Spencer disagreed with the opinion of Sir William Harcourt (home secretary) that 'there should be a respite until all the cases were disposed of, preferring to avoid delay if a commutation was clear'. Judge Murphy responded to Spencer's request in a hand-written report dated 8 August 1884. It stated that 'the evidence of the witness Raftery was in my opinion true in every particular. He was a perfectly untainted witness and his evidence alone was sufficient to establish prisoner's participation in the crime charged.'[7] Murphy claimed that Moran's evidence was proved by that of Raftery to be a 'particularly true narrative of all the circumstances immediately connected with the murder' and he accepted that Moran's evidence was corroborated by the Dohertys despite the many discrepancies exposed at the trials. In his conclusion the judge stated that 'it was a perfectly just verdict and any jury that did their duty were bound to find the prisoner guilty'.

The reply of the lord chancellor stated that 'Finnegan's conviction makes it advisable to consider the two cases together, but nothing seems to have occurred in Finnegan's trial adverse to the view of not carrying out the capital sentence on Muldowney'. On 8 August, Under Secretary Sir Robert Hamilton advised Spencer that the jury strongly recommended Finnegan to mercy, and the judge concurred. On receipt of the judge's report, the lord chancellor had a long interview with Judge Murphy, during which the judge strongly recommended the commutation of Finnegan's death sentence. Hamilton concluded by stating that 'the papers go over today to Althorp' with the chancellor's letter and that Spencer did not need to return to Dublin. There is no indication that either Spencer or the lord chancellor had transcripts of the evidence and it would appear therefore that they relied on the opinions of Judge Murphy. On 9 August, Spencer made the final decision, commuting the sentence of death on Muldowney to penal servitude for life. At that stage, even though he had decided to treat the two cases together, there was no announcement of a commutation for Finnegan.

In another letter to the home secretary, Spencer made an interesting comment: 'the attorney general who prosecuted the case said that, after seeing Muldowney, it was difficult to believe him capable of consenting and carrying out such a murder'.[8] If the attorney general believed that, he should have

lord chancellor 1883.   7 NAI CRF misc. 1903/396.   8 BL Spencer papers, 76933, Spencer to Harcourt, 19 Aug. 1884.

conducted a more critical examination of the evidence that condemned Muldowney to death. Following the return of Finnegan to Galway Jail, three police pensioners, William McGann, James Flannery and John Ahern, were employed to maintain a twenty-four hour watch on him. A special diet was recommended and permission was given for the Sisters of Mercy to visit the jail.[9] The controversy regarding the reply to the parliamentary question of Tim Healy[10] (see above, p. 65) continued following a letter from Thomas Finnegan, father of the prisoner.[11] The letter referred to the reply of the chief secretary to Healy's question, in which he had stated that the prisoners, through their solicitor and counsel, had offered to plead guilty to conspiracy to murder. This was branded 'a gross falsehood'; instead it was the crown that made the approach to the prisoners through their legal advisors and, despite strong pressure, the prisoners rejected the offer, declaring that, 'as they had no knowledge of the crime, they could not plead guilty to any offence'. The letter claimed that such conduct was unworthy of any government and it clearly showed the means adopted in Ireland to uphold the 'law'. It concluded by stating that 'Finnegan was offered his liberty and a very large sum of money, if he gave evidence against the other prisoners'. The solicitor general was challenged to publish the correspondence relating to this offer but there is no correspondence of this nature in the registered papers of Dublin Castle.

On 18 August, George Mason, the governor of Galway Jail, sent a memorial from Finnegan to Dublin Castle in which he solemnly declared that he did not commit the murder. Spencer ordered that the memorial be sent to Judge Murphy and asked the judge to meet him on 21 August. However, there is no record that such a meeting took place. On 19 August, in a letter to Sir William Harcourt, the home secretary, Spencer made the extraordinary claim that the witness Raftery joined an assassination society after the Doherty murder and was privy to the Blake murder. Presumably, Spencer was quoting from a police report. If that were the case, why did he not inform Judge Murphy, who had recently described Raftery as 'an untainted witness'? The veracity of the claim must be questioned, however, as it may have been an attempt by Raftery to convince the police that he had access to information about the Fenians and local agrarian societies. Given his local reputation, it is fanciful to believe that any Fenian group would have countenanced association with him. The letter also claimed that the commutation of Muldowney's sentence had given great satisfaction to the police and that the commutation had spread horror among the members of the secret society in Loughrea, 'who hoped for either the acquittal or the hanging of the two men. They think now they [Muldowney and Finnegan] will tell tales and are frightened to death'.[12]

9 NAI CSO RP 1884/10692, 10758 and 10818; all in CRF misc. 1903/396. 10 *Freeman's Journal*, 9 Aug. 1884. 11 *Tuam News*, 15 Aug. 1884; *Freeman's Journal*, 11 Aug. 1884. 12 BL Spencer papers, 76933, Spencer to Harcourt, 19 Aug. 1884.

PREPARATIONS FOR EXECUTION

During August 1884, preparations were made for the execution of three prisoners. Michael Tansey, convicted of the murder of William Mahon at Ballyforan, Co. Roscommon, in 1879,[13] was due to be hanged on 11 August, Michael Muldowney on the following day and Patrick Finnegan on 27 August. The executioner engaged for the hangings by the sheriff was James Berry (fig. 7, p. 77), a native of Heckmondwike, Yorkshire.

Berry had been a member of Bradford Borough Police for eight years before adopting his new profession. He regarded hanging as a business and whenever an execution was announced he applied to the sheriff of the county, enclosing his business card (fig. 8, p. 77). His business terms were ten guineas per person and 20s. for an assistant and he also claimed second-class rail fares.[14]

In his autobiography, he referred to several encounters on his rail journeys to and from Galway when he believed his life was in danger from dangerous characters that entered his carriage. On 8 August, Finnegan was removed under police escort from Sligo Jail and travelled as far as Mullingar, where he joined the Dublin–Galway train. On the train, his police guard introduced him to Berry and they travelled to Galway in the same carriage.[15] Berry wrote that in Galway 'he had nothing more lively to do than read the newspapers and walk about in the dreary prison yard, because the governor did not consider that it would be safe for me to venture outside'. Finnegan was not happy with Berry's presence, because he was given quarters directly above his cell and entertained himself by whistling and singing, which could be clearly heard by the condemned man.

On 22 August, Francis McCormick, Finnegan's defence solicitor, wrote to Dublin Castle requesting a commutation of the death sentence and he enclosed a memorial signed by eighteen citizens of Sligo city and county.[16] The memorial referred to the failure of the judge to accept a verdict of guilty to conspiracy and the jury's unanimous recommendation to mercy, which was based on the belief that it had not been proved that Finnegan actively participated in the offence but 'had been drawn into it by evil influences and by terror'. The signatories earnestly appealed that the lord lieutenant would mercifully commute the capital sentence. During the discussions between Spencer, Judge Murphy and the lord chancellor, the decision had been reached to commute the death sentence on both prisoners, but Finnegan was allowed to live under the threat of execution for a further fifteen days before Spencer appended his serpentine initial to the formal statement:

13 Joe Clarke, 'It's not fit for you to be keeping company with that unfortunate fellow' in Frank Sweeney (ed.), *Hanging crimes* (Cork, 2005), pp 168–202. 14 James Berry, *My experiences as an executioner*, ed. H. Snowden Ward (London, 1892). 15 *Boston Pilot*, 25 July 1903. 16 Signatories included Bernard Colleary, mayor of Sligo, three public representatives, Revd Richard McLaughlin, Revd John Corcoran, chaplain Sligo Jail, five justices of the peace and three members of juries in the trials of Muldowney and Finnegan.

7 (*left*) Executioner
James Berry, from
James Berry, *My
experiences as an
executioner*, ed. H.
Snowden Ward
(London, 1892).

8 (*below*) Business
card of James Berry,
executioner. From
Berry, *My experiences
as an executioner*.

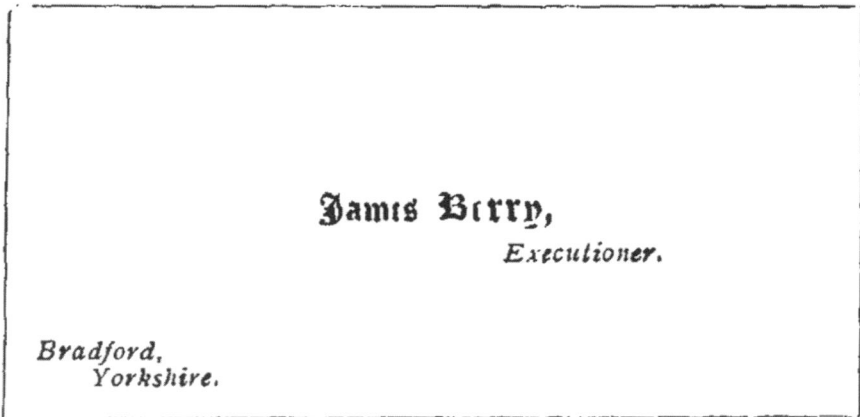

James Berry,
Executioner.

*Bradford,
   Yorkshire.*

'Having regard to the recommendation of the learned judge, I commute the sentence of death to penal servitude for life' (fig. 9). The recommendation of mercy made by the juries at the end of the trials was important because Vaughan's

Death Case

F. 32 : 188 4 .

APPLICATION FOR DISCHARGE OF A PRISONER.

County of ...   .   *Galway*

Name of Prisoner, ...   *Patrick Finnegan*

Before whom tried, ...   *Mr Justice Murphy.*

Whether pleaded Guilty or not Guilty?   *Not Guilty.*

Offence, ...   *Murder*

Sentence, ...   *To be hanged on 27th August 1884*

Date of Conviction   ...   ...   *6th August 1884.*

~~Date from which Sentence takes effect~~ .

Memorial on behalf of the Convict annexed.
The former papers were submitted on the 19th instant.

Submitted 22.8.84

Having regard to the recommendation of the jury & the support given to this recommendation by the learned judge I commute the sentence of death to Penal Servitude for life.

23.8.84

9 The commutation document, initialled by Lord Spencer (National Archives of Ireland Convict Reference File, Miscellaneous 1903; image reproduced courtesy of the Director of the National Archives of Ireland).

analysis[17] showed that 'two-thirds of the prisoners whom juries recommended to mercy were not hanged'. Muldowney and Tansey were removed to Mountjoy Jail on 15 August 1884,[18] and Finnegan followed on 28 August.

THE TRIAL OF MICHAEL FOGARTY, CARRICK-ON-SHANNON, WINTER ASSIZES, 1884

Interest in the fate of the remaining prisoners remained high and, in preparation for the trials at the winter assizes, the collection for the Prisoners' Defence Fund continued in south Galway. A further public appeal was made in early December for the purpose of engaging counsel for the defence of the prisoners. Posters were prominently displayed and signed by Revd B. Quinn, PP Craughwell, Poor Law Guardian Patrick Cawley, John Cunniffe, Patrick Barrett and Thomas Spellman.[19]

The trial of Michael Fogarty (Ballywinna) commenced on 8 December 1884 before Judge James Lawson[20] at Carrick-on-Shannon. Having opted out of the second Finnegan trial, George Orme Malley rejoined as defence counsel along with McDonnell Bodkin. The crown was represented by Sergeant Robinson QC and The McDermot QC. Introducing the case for the crown, Sergeant Robinson alleged that in 1880 Jack Moran, the approver, had been sworn into 'the Patriotic Brotherhood, what he supposed was called the Fenian Confederacy'. In stating the case for the defence, Malley made some extraordinary references to the previous convictions, for example:

> he was not there to say whether Muldowney and Finnegan had been rightly convicted. The assumption should be that the verdict was right; but with regard to them, the evidence was more clear, conclusive and convincing than anything that could be brought against the prisoner at the Bar.

It is difficult to understand how Malley, having heard the evidence at several trials and having read the depositions of witnesses, could not have been aware of the dubious nature of Moran's claims and the perjury committed by him. The comments may also explain why Malley failed to attend for the second trial of Finnegan and the pressure that Malley and the defence solicitor exerted on the prisoners to plead guilty to a charge of conspiracy to murder. Yet, Malley went

---

17 Vaughan, *Murder trials in Ireland*, p. 315.   18 *Galway Vindicator*, 16 Aug. 1884.   19 *Tuam News*, 5 Dec. 1884.   20 James Anthony Lawson, solicitor general, 1861–5, AG 1865–6, judge of the court of common pleas, 1868–82, and judge of the queen's bench division, 1882–7. According to Vaughan (*Murder trials in Ireland*, p. 258), although Lawson supported the abolition of capital punishment, he condemned 14 prisoners to death, 8 of whom were hanged. He was uninjured in an attempted assassination by the Invincibles on 11 Nov. 1882 (T. Corfe, *The Phoenix Park murders*, London, 1968, pp 233–5).

on to challenge the 'clear, conclusive and convincing evidence' stating that the whole case against Fogarty 'depended on the evidence of two witnesses, Raftery and Moran and ... if they had any doubt of the evidence of Raftery and if they had no confidence in the evidence of Moran, they were bound to acquit the prisoner'. He claimed that Raftery's identification of Fogarty as one of the shooting party was insufficient and that the evidence of Moran was wholly unworthy of credit. This was precisely the case in the trials of Muldowney, in which no corroborative evidence was presented other than Raftery's and, in the case of Finnegan's trials, the corroboration by the Dohertys was of the flimsiest nature.

The evidence presented at Fogarty's trial was essentially the same as in the earlier trials. Margaret Raftery stated that her husband was at home 'all the evening of the murder and that she knew what her husband had told was a lie'.[21] John Ryder said that, to the best of his belief, Fogarty was in his house on the night of the murder, and Martin Cloonan supported this statement. The McDermot made the closing remarks for the crown. He claimed that the story told by Moran was true, but that it relied heavily on the evidence of Raftery for corroboration. Judge Lawson gave a more balanced analysis of the evidence on this occasion than Judge Murphy's account at the earlier trials. He said that 'if the case rested on the evidence of Moran alone, it would be their bounden duty to acquit the prisoner and if they believed Raftery they should find a verdict of guilty'.[22] In his summary, Judge Lawson referred to the evidence for the defence and stated that it contained claims that neither Moran nor Raftery were at the scene of the murder, and that Fogarty also was in another place. His lordship then said that if any reasonable doubt was on their minds, they should find a verdict of acquittal.[23]

The jury retired at 7pm, and at 9.15pm one of the jurors said that some members wished to know if they could find a verdict on Raftery's evidence alone. The judge replied 'if you believe him'. This would indicate that some of the jurors had doubts about the evidence of Moran. Another juror asked whether a minor indictment might be considered and Judge Lawson responded that if they did not agree he would discharge them. A juror then stated that they could not agree and the judge discharged them. The cases were adjourned to the spring assizes and the prisoners were remanded in custody.

By early March 1885, the defence solicitor had received no notice of a retrial, but when the spring assizes opened on 6 March The McDermot QC, representing the crown, entered a plea of *nolle prosequi* and all four prisoners (Fogarty, Joyce, Connolly and Conway) were released.[24] It is an eloquent judgment on the crown's case that the evidence that condemned two people to death was now considered to be insufficient to try the others.

21 *Tuam News*, 26 Dec. 1884. 22 Ibid. 23 Ibid. 24 *Freeman's Journal*, 7 Mar. 1885.

On their arrival at Athenry station, large crowds, led by the Athenry Temperance Band, greeted the prisoners, who had spent twenty-six months in jail from the time of their arrest in January 1883. Bonfires blazed at every cross-roads on their journey to Craughwell, where an enthusiastic crowd of about one thousand people greeted the prisoners before conveying them to their homes. The homecoming was associated with sadness for two of the released men because of the deaths of John Conway's mother and Michael Connolly's father while they were in prison.

THE AFTERMATH OF THE KILLING FOR THE DOHERTY FAMILY

The compensation hearing relating to the death of Peter Doherty took place in Galway Record Court before Mr J. Alexander Byrne QC in November 1882. The claim was lodged by his father, Peter Doherty Senior, who stated that Peter Junior was his only son and he had two daughters, Kate and Mary Anne. His wife, Margaret, had died on 6 December 1881, four weeks after the death of her son. Prior to taking the boycotted land, he had a farm of twelve acres with five cattle, twenty sheep and two horses. His son took extra land – four acres for meadow and oats and conacre for potatoes. When he and his cousin took the disputed land, stones were thrown through the windows, the tail was cut off the horse and some of the fences and about thirty yards of a stone wall were broken down. After the killing of his son, he had given up the disputed land and was unable to get anyone to help with his own holding. Local blacksmiths refused to shoe the horse and he had to take the horse to Athenry to have it shod. Kate Doherty, referring to the shooting of her brother, said that she saw 'the shadows of some men but did not see their persons.'

The judge thought that a sum should be provided that was sufficient for good fortunes for the two girls and the award amounted to £600. In fact, Mary Anne Doherty married a man called Hubert Flannon from Creggs, Co. Roscommon, on 15 September 1884,[25] soon after the conviction of Finnegan and Muldowney. The family were subjected to intimidation in the form of threatening letters and verbal abuse and all the members of both Peter Doherty's and John Doherty's families emigrated to America.[26]

Writing to the *Tuam Herald*, Finnegan's friend Michael Clasby described how Pat Martin, a visitor from San Francisco, travelled to Carrigan and inter-viewed John Doherty, who made a statement witnessed by John Connolly, Carrigan. The statement was given to John Sweeney, the well known nationalist from Loughrea, who, prior to his death, entrusted it to Clasby.[27] Doherty's state-ment was as follows:

---

25 Record in marriage register in Craughwell church, courtesy of Maura Lyons.   26 NAI ILL and INL documents, carton 10.   27 Sweeney, who died in 1899, could not have known that following his release Finnegan would marry his daughter Alice.

I am now going to leave with my family for the USA and I, being one of the injured parties, state most positively that I believe Pat Finnegan is innocent of the crime of assassinating Peter Doherty. I therefore wish to leave behind me this statement in order that it may be of some future benefit to him whom I believe to be innocent of the crime he is now suffering for.[28]

THE LATER LIVES OF REDINGTON AND BELL

The Loughrea correspondent of the *Tuam News* observed that the crown must have been fully aware that the convictions of Muldowney and Finnegan were obtained by perjury and fraud. He also castigated Redington, now promoted to Sergeant,[29] for his role in the case, alleging that he had offered money to Mrs Raftery to swear contrary to her earlier depositions.[30] Redington was further rewarded later when he was appointed DI in Co. Longford.

The main orchestrator of the prosecution case against Muldowney and Finnegan had been SI Alan Bell, who was stationed at Athenry. He was soon promoted to become DI as a result of the diligent pursuit of his duties. Bell was the son of a Church of Ireland clergyman and he was born in Banagher, King's County (Offaly). He joined the RIC in 1879 and served in Ballyconnell, Co. Cavan, before transfer to Athenry. Later postings in his career in the RIC were in Athlone, Mallow and Mullingar. He was appointed RM in 1898 and served in Lurgan and Portadown. In late 1919, he was transferred to Dublin Castle for the purpose of investigating the financial affairs of the IRA and to identify the banking services used by Michael Collins to fund the War of Independence. Raids on Sinn Féin offices produced evidence relating to the bank accounts, and Bell commenced proceedings against officials of the Hibernian and Munster and Leinster Banks.[31] Michael Collins viewed Bell's activities with alarm and a decision was made to assassinate him. On 25 March 1920, Bell left his home in Monkstown, Co. Dublin, to travel by tram to Dublin Castle. As the tram passed through Ballsbridge, Bell was overpowered by a gang of armed men, taken from the tram and shot dead on the roadway. An eye-witness said that he saw the men approach Bell, who was reading a morning newspaper, and one of them tapped him on the shoulder saying 'come on, Mister Bell, your time has come'. Three shots rang out, killing him instantly.[32] The post mortem examination revealed three bullet wounds, in the right temple, left groin and left wrist. The burial took place in Deansgrange cemetery on 30 March 1920.[33]

28 *Tuam Herald*, 1 Sept. 1900. 29 *Tuam News*, 5 Dec. 1884. 30 *Tuam News*, 13 Mar. 1885.
31 Peter Hart, *Mick* (London, 2005), p. 196; Tim Pat Coogan, *The man who made Ireland* (London, 1990), p. 188 and Michael T. Foy, *Michael Collins's intelligence war* (Stroud, 2006), pp 81–2. 32 *Irish Times*, 26 Mar. 1920. 33 *Irish Times*, 29 Mar. 1920.

THE ROLE AND FATE OF THE CROWN WITNESSES

The trial of the Maamtrasna prisoners is probably the best known example of the role of the crown witness during the Land War. The Prevention of Crime (Ireland) Act of 1882 allowed, as we have seen, for the changing of the venues of trials to ensure a more compliant jury and the packing of juries by careful selection in order to achieve this end. There are clear parallels between the Maamtrasna trials and the trials of the Craughwell prisoners. The Maamtrasna trials were transferred from Galway to the Dublin Commission and the Craughwell trials from Galway to Sligo, in both cases in order to obtain verdicts from carefully selected lists of jurors. Both trials featured the evidence of approvers, Anthony Philbin, who knew nothing of the murders, Thomas Casey, who participated in the Maamtrasna killings, and Jack Moran, who was helplessly drunk and miles away from the scene of the Doherty killing. Evidence that by any standard was highly suspect was described as 'clearly and conclusively' establishing guilt in both cases. The fact that James Murphy was the chief crown prosecutor in the Maamtrasna case and judge in the other cases explains the recurring phraseology. The resulting execution of the innocent Myles Joyce was an outcome narrowly averted in the cases of Muldowney and Finnegan, whose sentences of death were commuted. Precisely at the time of the Craughwell trials, July–August of 1884, Thomas Casey made a public retraction of his perjured evidence in Tourmakeady Church, Co. Mayo. Despite parliamentary debate and criticism and public clamour for justice, the authorities obdurately refused to 'reopen the subject'. Lord Spencer believed that the verdict and sentences were right and just, and consequently declined to 'interfere with the course of the law'.[34] The Craughwell prisoners were also unfortunate that the evidence of the disreputable informers was first of all tutored carefully by the police and then accepted as fact by the establishment figure of Judge James Murphy and the 'packed' Sligo juries.

An interesting insight into the system emerges from the treatment of the crown witnesses in the case of the Craughwell prisoners. The principal informers were Patrick (Patsy) Raftery and John (Jack) Moran, but the chief secretary's files reveal the involvement of two others who made statements about the accused men. James Gavin, who had earlier offered evidence in relation to the Letterfrack conspiracy case, and, in a bizarre coincidence, another John Moran, a witness in the Tubbercurry conspiracy case. Neither man had any direct connection with the Craughwell case, but they became acquainted with the Craughwell prisoners in jail and informed the authorities about conversations they allegedly had with them.

---

34 Spencer papers, 77318A. Memo printed in relation to House of Commons debate.

Patrick Raftery and John (Jack) Moran

Although Raftery did not give his first sworn deposition until 17 February 1883, he was under the protection of the police from 26 January. He was given lodgings in Galway under the protection of Constable R. Hughes, who, on 16 February, reported to SI W. Lennon that he had found a coat, trousers, vest and shirt for him at a cost of £1 10s. 0d. In April 1883, Raftery and Moran were lodged in a large detached house in Ballybough, known as the crown witness depot. A second crown witness depot was situated at Kingscourt House, Clontarf, and DI Heard of the Crime Branch at Dublin Castle was responsible for all matters relating to both establishments. When their presence was required in Galway for magisterial hearings, Raftery and Moran stayed in lodgings in Woodquay. They were both in poor health; in Moran's case this was probably alcohol related and Raftery suffered from chronic asthma. On 17 May, HC Wynne submitted a red ticket that entitled Moran to free dispensary care. It was promptly returned by Dr P.M. Rice of Millbrook House, who stated that Moran was not entitled to dispensary relief because 'he is neither destitute, a pauper nor a poor person'.[35] However, medical attention was arranged for both witnesses with Dr Rice, who was willing to accept a fee of 10s. per visit. Requests for the payment of expenses and for the purchase of clothing were submitted to the inspector general of the RIC at regular intervals throughout 1883 and 1884. Moran's family were also accorded police protection and, for a period, Maria Moran and her children were in England, returning to Ireland in August 1883 and staying for one night in Gort Workhouse before they were accommodated elsewhere.[36]

In August 1884, following the conviction of Muldowney and Finnegan, the police thought it was no longer safe for Raftery to stay in Galway and he was transferred to Armagh. On 13 August, Captain Gregg, who was in charge of Raftery, reported that he was very ill with asthma and, two weeks later, DI Samuel Waters stated that Dr Robert Gray was quite willing to attend any crown witness at the rate of 10s. per visit.[37] There were regular authorizations for expenses, maintenance and clothes for both Raftery and Moran, and in January 1884 Moran's wife Maria and their four children joined him in Ballybough. Thereafter, the family were maintained at a cost of 6s. 7d. per day.[38] On 3 June, the chief secretary approved the appointment of a midwife to attend Mrs Moran and their fifth child was born in August.[39]

The 'disposal' of Patrick Raftery

Discussions on the 'disposal' of Raftery commenced after the failure to agree a verdict in the Fogarty trial in December 1884. DI Alan Bell wrote to the county inspector in Ballinasloe stating that Raftery was very anxious that his eldest son,

35 NAI CSO RP 1883/12550. 36 *Tuam News*, 17 Aug. 1883. 37 NAI CSO RP 1888/13481. 38 NAI CSO RP 1884/25542 in 1885/5456. 39 NAI CSO RP 1884/12864.

John, aged 9 years, would join him when the time came for his departure overseas. The child was living with his mother, Margaret, 'who is very hostile to her husband since he became a crown witness and … she took every opportunity of insulting her husband when she sees him'. Raftery asked if he could travel to Rahasane, under escort, to talk to his son, but Attorney General John Naish rejected the proposal.[40] In March 1885, when the trials were abandoned, DM Andrew Reed, in a letter to the under secretary, reported the hostility of Raftery's wife Margaret, who 'refuses to have anything further to do with her husband'. Raftery was now 34 years old and had to leave his home and three children when he became a crown witness. Reed stated that he had made every endeavour to affect reconciliation between them, 'hoping that the whole family might be induced to emigrate – but without success'. Reed claimed that Mrs Raftery had 'been aided by the Nationalist Party' and he further stated that he had experienced difficulty in persuading Raftery to emigrate without his family, but 'if he were to remain in the United Kingdom he would require constant police protection'. Consultations took place between DM Andrew Reed, RM A.N. Brady, DI Alan Bell and CI Byrne, and they agreed that '£500 would not be too large a sum to expend'. Reed was anxious to reduce the 'expense to as low a limit as possible'. Further discussion reduced the sum to £300 to include the travel expenses to Australia, where Raftery wished to go, and would also provide financial support for his children. The final agreement was that Raftery would be paid £150, out of which he would pay all expenses of emigration (£17 18s.) and outfit (£15 18s. 6d.) and the sum of £16 3s. 6d. was given to him as cash and also a bank draft payable in Melbourne for £100. He was promised a further payment of £50, to be paid in Melbourne twelve months after his arrival, provided he did not return home. Reed stated that 'it would never do to emigrate Raftery and leave his children on the parish and the Nationalist Party would no doubt take up the case and demand from the government that provision be made for the family'. Reed claimed that the Nationalist Party was supporting Mrs Raftery but, if so, the support cannot have been generous because she had to apply to Gort Poor Law Union in May 1885 for support for herself and her family.[41] Reed concluded by remarking that 'if my proposals are granted, this witness will be disposed of most economically'. Raftery expressed himself very grateful for the provision recommended for his children. This fund amounted to £100, payable in instalments of £12 annually. At the conclusion of payments, therefore, his youngest child would have reached the age of eleven. Mrs Raftery was given £6 for the period up to 31 December and Revd P.A. McDonagh, PP Clarinbridge, sent a receipt for the payment to Dublin Castle.[42]

40 NAI CSO RP 1884/27974 in 1888/13481, Bell to William Jones, 24 Dec. 1884. **41** *Tuam News*, 17 Apr. 1885. **42** NAI CSO RP 1885/13252 in 1888/13481, Reed to under secretary, 15 July 1885.

The financial arrangements were completed in Galway on 29 August and Raftery sailed for Melbourne on 2 October 1885. It has not been possible to trace his arrival in Australia or his ultimate fate.

The 'disposal' of John (Jack) Moran

During March 1885, Jack Moran and his family were living in the crown witness depot at Kingscourt House, the depot in Ballybough having been condemned as unsuitable. DM Andrew Reed reported to the under secretary on 24 March that Moran gave evidence of vital importance in the Craughwell case and his wife corroborated as regards collateral matters. Interestingly, he added that the Morans had 'given useful information with reference to other matters affecting the peace of the Co. Galway'. This would suggest that the police in Craughwell might have known whom to approach for information regarding the Doherty killing. In customary manner, Reed held consultations and agreement was reached that Moran deserved a grant of £200 to enable him to emigrate and provide a home for his family in another country.[43] Reed further commented that Moran would have to emigrate, as 'life would not be safe in Ireland unless he received constant police protection'.

In the latter part of the nineteenth century, there were public protests regarding the dispatch of convicted criminals to the colonies.[44] Writing from the colonial office, Robert Herbert informed Dublin Castle that the Cape government would be sure to object to the immigration of criminals and Lord Derby 'would therefore not wish to have any informers (even of a mild type) sent to any of the self-governing colonies'.[45] Moran, therefore, could not be sent to a colony because he was tainted with crime and so arrangements were made to send himself and his wife and family to San Francisco.

DI Heard provided an itemized account of the disbursements for the purchase of clothes for the family and the cost of travel. The cost of the passage to New York was £52 10s., the rail fare to San Francisco was £5 13s. 9d, and £10 was spent on clothing. The family travelled to Londonderry by train accompanied by Constable A. Jones, who also supervized their embarkation at Moville; they sailed from there on 24 May 1885.[46] On departure, Jack Moran was handed a draft drawn on a bank in San Francisco for £125 and he adopted the new identity of John Joseph O'Kelly.

There was no communication from Moran for ten years, until a letter, dated 4 February 1895, arrived in Dublin Castle revealing that he was now in New Westminster Prison, British Columbia. Moran described himself as destitute,

---

43 NAI CSO RP 1885/5456, Reed to under secretary, 24 Mar. 1885.   44 John Mitchel, in ch. xi of the *Jail journal* (Dublin, 1914) gives a detailed account of a protest against the landing of convicts in Cape Town that he witnessed while in transit from Bermuda to Tasmania in 1849. 45 NAI CSO RP 1884/18502, Herbert to Jenkinson.   46 NAI CSO RP 1885/8658 in 1897/1602, Jones to Heard, 1 May 1885.

old and unable to work. He had committed a crime so as to be sent to jail, as he had no other place to go.[47] Moran stated that he had to give up his trade after leaving San Francisco, 'owing to parties following me'. He claimed that 'his misfortune was all owing to his wife leaving him and selling all he had'. He had to leave Victoria, British Columbia, when a newspaper reported that he was an informer and as 'bad as Carey, one of the Phoenix Park assassins'. 'In every corner of the town, I was called informer and had to leave'. He expressed the wish to be admitted to an old people's home in the province, although at this stage he was only 50 years old. He concluded by stating that the government had told him that 'they never would see me short, now is the time or never. If I was as loyal to the other side as I was to the government I never would be short'. His parting remark was 'No more your obedient servant, John Kelly'. On receipt of the letter, the under secretary, Sir David Harrell, asked the attorney general whether an answer should be given. The attorney general, The McDermot QC (who acted for the prosecution in the Doherty trials), responded that Moran 'had been liberally treated in 1885 and on terms intended to be final. Yet if Moran can be got into an institution for old men – it would be an act of benevolence'. The chief secretary, John Morley, endorsed this sentiment, but no action on the suggestion is recorded in the files.

Almost two years later, a letter arrived from Vina del Mar, Chile, a seaside suburb of Valparaiso. 'I take the liberty to send you a note from the poor house (Hospicio) in this country'. Moran reported that he had boarded a lumber ship in British Columbia bound for Chile. However, he did not know the language and was unable to obtain employment; he slept out at night and he was often hungry. He repeated the account of his wife telling people he was an informer and claimed he was fired at in British Columbia. He stated that he was sure his friends in Ireland would be glad of his downfall. Moran pleaded for five or six dollars a month that could be sent to the English consul general in Valparaiso who knew he was in the home. The money would allow him to buy tobacco and bread. As an alternative, he requested an opportunity to return to England. The attorney general and the chief secretary, Gerald William Balfour, agreed that no reply should be sent.[48] Although Moran's fate is a sad one, it is difficult to conjure much sympathy for a man whose perjury condemned two innocent men to death.

James Fox

A third crown witness, James Fox, the coachman at Rahasane House, was given support from 18 February 1883 and was maintained in Manchester throughout the investigations and trials. Correspondence with Alan Bell indicates that Fox was far from happy with his lot as a crown witness. In July 1884, Bell wrote to

47 NAI CSO RP 1895/3082 in 1897/1602. 48 NAI CSO RP 1897/1602.

Dublin Castle stating that Fox had applied for a suit of clothes and although he was allocated one pound expenses per week, Fox complained that he was not always paid promptly. Bell reported that Fox had 'lost three different employments during the progress of this case, owing to his having to come over from Manchester to every assizes and he is now out of employment'. After the convictions of Muldowney and Finnegan, DI William Jones applied for support for Fox as an important witness in the trials of the remaining prisoners. Jones claimed that if Fox was not supported 'he may go to join his wife in America'. Thereafter, expenses were paid until the trials were abandoned in March 1885 and, at that stage, DM Andrew Reed wrote to the under secretary recommending Fox's discharge. Reed consulted CS Thomas D. Farrell, CI Byrne, RM A.N. Brady and DI Alan Bell and they agreed to recommend that Fox should receive £30. The attorney general, John Naish, approved this. The payment was justified by the fact that Fox had lost his employment and had been prevented from joining his wife in America.[49] Fox's reward was paltry recompense for almost two years of separation from his wife and the loss of his employment.[50] He almost certainly emigrated to America to join his wife, but it has not been possible to trace his subsequent career.

THE LETTERFRACK MURDER CONSPIRACY AND TRIALS

Although two informers were instrumental in achieving the convictions of Muldowney and Finnegan, the Dublin Castle papers reveal the existence of two other men who were prepared to give incriminating evidence in their trials. The individuals were James Gavin from Currywongane, Letterfrack, and another man named John Moran from Tubbercurry.

On 24 April 1881, John Lyden and his son Martin were shot dead at their home near Letterfrack as a result of an agrarian dispute. The Lydens worked as herds for a Mr Graham and they also acquired property from Graham that was previously rented by a man called Patrick Walsh. Walsh was arrested as a suspect in relation to the murder of the Lydens and his trial was transferred to the Dublin Commission in August 1882. He was found guilty and hanged in Galway Jail on 22 September 1882. On 15 February 1882, Constable James Kavanagh was shot dead near Letterfrack Police Barracks. He had been active in procuring evidence against Patrick Walsh and Walsh's son Michael was arrested and convicted for the killing at the Dublin Commission in September 1882. He was condemned to death, but the sentence was commuted to penal servitude for life.[51] James Gavin had been present at the trial of Michael Walsh as a witness for the defence, but there is no record in newspaper accounts that he was called

49 NAI CSO RP 1885/4827 in 1888/13481. 50 Ibid. 51 NAI CSO RP 1891/28047.

to give evidence. In July 1883, he approached the police and claimed that he had been sworn into the Letterfrack secret society by two of the conspirators and, in his statement, he named a large number of alleged members of the society. He also named the alleged members of the party that shot Lyden. The Letterfrack trial was held in December 1883 at the Sligo winter assizes, where the prisoners pleaded guilty to conspiracy to murder. Prison sentences of ten years were imposed on four of the accused. Four others were given sentences of twelve to eighteen months. Because the accused pleaded guilty, James Gavin was not called to give evidence.[52] On 13 December 1883, Constable Patrick Hayes wrote to Alan Bell stating that, when he was returning from the Letterfrack trial, he had a conversation with James Gavin, who told him that he became acquainted with the Craughwell prisoners while he was in Galway Jail between March and September 1883. At that time, he was a prisoner charged with stealing cattle from his uncle. Gavin claimed that the Craughwell prisoners 'told him the part they took in the Doherty murder'.[53] The following day, Bell wrote to DM Andrew Reed urging that a statement be taken from Gavin at once and he suggested 'that Gavin be not finally disposed of or receive any payment till this statement be considered fully'.[54] Reed asked DI Phillips for his opinion and he replied that he thought it was highly improbable that the prisoners would make any disclosures to a stranger and a young fellow like Gavin;[55] nevertheless he agreed to interview him later that month. This interview took place at the crown witness depot in Kingscourt House, Clontarf. Gavin said he had a conversation with Finnegan when they were in adjacent cells and that Finnegan had 'asked him if he was right, meaning was he a member of a secret society, and Gavin replied that he was'. Gavin asked Finnegan if all the fellows who were in with him were 'right' and he acknowledged that they were. Gavin then alleged that Finnegan confessed to the murder. Gavin also stated that Thomas Joyce told him that it was not the first thing that Michael Connolly had done and that Joyce also referred to being in the public house before the murder. Gavin further claimed that Muldowney had asked him what he was doing in the Governor's office and that he replied 'that the police were asking me what I knew about the Letterfrack case'. He reported that Muldowney said in reply 'not to tell them anything, that informers were badly treated and that the fellow who swore him was a bloody informer what himself [Muldowney] would never be'. This exchange has a ring of truth and indicates the sense of vulnerability and suspicion aroused by the sight of fellow prisoners making visits to the governor's office to be interviewed by police and crown law officers. DI Phillips concluded his report by stating that 'Gavin is very young and, seeing that he is now branded as an informer, he wants to push himself into another crown case'. Phillips stated that he 'did not think

52 *Freeman's Journal*, 11 Dec. 1883.   53 NAI CSO RP 1884/18360 Hayes to Bell, 13 Dec. 1883.
54 NAI CSO RP 1884/5830 in 1884/18360, Bell to Reed, 14 Dec. 1883.   55 NAI CSO RP 1883/28410, Phillips to Reed, 18 Dec. 1883.

any jury would believe his statement and I would not think it prudent or advisable to produce him in this case'. The attorney general, John Naish, clearly agreed, because in a marginal note he wrote 'I do not trust this statement, but it will be well not to lose Gavin'.[56]

DI Alan Bell was indefatigable in his determination to have the Craughwell prisoners convicted and he believed that Gavin 'could not possibly have invented his story'. He claimed that Muldowney had a reason for his remarks about informers as he had been interviewed by HC Wynne who advised him to tell all he knew, but Muldowney refused. In a second statement, taken by Sergeant R. Jones on 22 January 1884, Gavin said that he made a mistake in his statement to DI Phillips about the party leaving Cunniffe's house, that it was in Cawley's house they met Muldowney. He added that some of them went along with Muldowney on the car to Doherty's house and that more of them made a short cut. Bell gave his opinion that, because Gavin made statements that were not in line with the evidence given by Raftery and Moran, this meant that he could not have been tutored about its contents and that he was telling the truth.[57] The contents of the witness depositions of Raftery and Moran must have been a common topic of conversation in Galway Jail while the prisoners awaited trial and it would appear likely that Gavin was merely reporting a garbled version of what he heard.

On receipt of DI Bell's communication, DM Andrew Reed instructed him to ascertain if Finnegan was in the next cell to Gavin. Bell met the governor of Galway Jail, who informed him that the prisoners constantly conversed with one another by means of the pipes that ran through the cells and acted as a telephone. The warder reported that there were three cells between Gavin and Finnegan but there was no comment on whether or not they could communicate at that distance.[58] The documents were seen by the attorney general, who commented 'I do not much like this class of evidence and think it will be better not to use it'. Discussions took place in April 1884 regarding arrangements for the emigration of Gavin, but Bell continued his efforts to have Gavin produced as a witness.[59] Acting on the verbal instructions of Samuel Anderson,[60] DI Bell and DI Joyce obtained another statement from Gavin on 25 April.[61] Bell commented that the manner of the witness convinced them of the truth of the statement and, if 'put in evidence at the trials, would corroborate the evidence of Jack Moran'. On this occasion, Gavin's allegations were at variance with the statement of 22 January. He now claimed that Finnegan told him that they met in Cunniffe's public house from where they went to Cawley's, where they met Muldowney. He said that

56 NAI CSO RP 1884/48, Phillips to Reed, 29 Dec. 1883.   57 NAI CSO RP 1884/18360, Bell to Reed, 26 Feb. 1884.   58 NAI CSO RP 1884/18360, Bell to Reed, 26 & 28 Feb. 1884.   59 NAI CSO RP 1884/7355.   60 Samuel Lee Anderson, assistant under secretary, police and crime.   61 DI William Henry Joyce was asked to join the divisional special branch by DM Andrew Reed.

Regan supplied the arms and they returned the arms to Regan after the murder. There were no references to any of the other prisoners, but nevertheless DI Joyce was 'perfectly satisfied that he is telling the truth' and strongly recommended that Gavin be retained until after the trial. He advised taking Gavin to Sligo Jail and

> having his deposition taken in the presence of Finnegan, which might have the effect of inducing him (Finnegan) to turn approver. This would be of immense importance, as in all probability it would lead up to the detection of other serious crimes which have been perpetrated in the same locality, which is one of the worst parts of the Co. Galway.[62]

This comment is of interest because Finnegan was approached during the trials and offered a reward and a pardon if he gave evidence against the other prisoners.[63] The attorney general again commented that Gavin's evidence should not be relied upon or used in the case.[64]

Nevertheless, the attorney general instructed DI Joyce to take a further statement from Gavin and this was done on 28 June at Clontarf. Gavin again repeated the contact with Finnegan, who was in the next cell for a short time and later in the cell opposite, when they were able to talk to each other under the door. Finnegan allegedly told him that the party met in Cunniffe's and that it was on Cunniffe's behalf that they shot Doherty. Gavin said that he spoke to Muldowney in the water closet on the day he gave information on the Letterfrack case to DI Phillips and HC Colligan and that Muldowney said he heard that Gavin was giving evidence and told him 'never to do that – that it was better to be transported for life than to be an informer, that the man that swore him in was an informer, and that he would never become one'. The version of Moran's story contained in Gavin's statements would suggest that the statements were merely hearsay garnered from prisoners other than the accused who stoutly maintained their innocence of the crime throughout the trials and subsequently. It is not surprising, therefore, that the attorney general refused to use Gavin's evidence in court and he was not called as a witness in the trials of Muldowney and Finnegan at the Sligo summer assizes.

Gavin had consented to emigrate in April 1884 and the government had agreed to grant him a sum of £100.[65] On 16 April, Gavin wrote to Samuel Anderson, stating that he had been accepted as an approver in the Letterfrack case and that he now wished to be compensated and discharged at an early time. Gavin stated that, as he was the principal witness in the case, he expected to be dealt with liberally. The following day, he received a letter from his mother,

62 NAI CSO RP 1884/10093 in 1884/18360. **63** *Freeman's Journal*, 11 Aug. 1884; *Tuam News*, 15 Aug. 1884. **64** NAI CSO RP 1884/15544 in 1885/5161, Joyce to attorney general, 29 June 1884. **65** NAI CSO RP 1884/7355, Reed to Jenkinson, 9 Apr. 1884.

relating that the family were leaving Westport and she requested money in order to purchase clothes. Gavin sent this letter to Anderson, requesting £30, and he also asked for his own passage and that of Bridget Curley, who had consented to go with him. In August a letter from Gavin's father confirmed that the family had arrived in Canada and were living in Ayr, Ontario, and that three of the children were working.[66] Immediately after Finnegan's conviction, arrangements were made to send Gavin to Canada by O'Dell & Co. of Eden Quay, Dublin. An outfit of clothes was purchased for him and the fare from Londonderry to Toronto cost £5 6s. 7d., leaving a balance of £86 2s. 9d.; this amount was given to Gavin as a bank draft in the name of James Morrissy, his assumed name. He sailed for Canada on 22 August 1884.[67]

THE TUBBERCURRY CONSPIRACY CASE

P.N. Fitzgerald, a native of Cork, was the chief organizer of the IRB in Munster and he also became the organizer for Connacht when P.J. Sheridan was expelled from the IRB. He and John O'Connor were involved in the importation of arms.[68] Fitzgerald was arrested in London on 10 April 1884 and taken to Sligo Jail to be charged in connection with the Tubbercurry conspiracy to murder case.[69] He remained in Sligo Jail until he was tried at the Dublin Commission in November 1884 on a charge of treason felony. John Moran from Tubbercurry who was also arrested in connection with the case, had elected to become an approver. Previously, Moran had given information to the police that led to the seizure of arms; for this he was paid £5 'as an encouragement to find information regarding recent serious outrages in Tubbercurry'.[70]

Moran had been arrested in April 1883 and was on remand in Sligo Jail during June, when the Craughwell prisoners were confined there for the summer assizes. It would appear that he volunteered to give information and the attorney general instructed DI Joyce to interview him, which he did at Clontarf on 28 June. Moran claimed that he spoke to Muldowney during exercise and that Muldowney gave him a Fenian sign; that Muldowney admitted he was a sworn Fenian before he joined the force and that he 'knew Daly and Sheridan as Fenian organizers in his place in Co. Leitrim'. Moran alleged that Muldowney knew the murder was to be committed but that he and the man he was minding (Regan) remained drinking in the public house until after the murder had taken place. Moran also spoke to the other prisoners and they gave him the Fenian signs. He claimed that they all said 'they knew Fitzgerald when they saw him at Mass in the jail and that he had been around their part of the country with Sheridan

66 NAI CSO RP 1884/18360.   67 Ibid.   68 Owen McGee, *The IRB* (Dublin, 2005), pp 78–9.
69 *Freeman's Journal*, 12 Apr. 1884.   70 NAI CSO RP 1882/11767 in 1884/25599. SI F.W.
Gardener to CI T. Ross, 25 Mar. 1882.

organizing'. Other allegations made by Moran were that Finnegan told him that he, Joyce and Connolly fired the shots; Connolly admitted being there, Fogarty said he knew all about it and Conway said he was in the public house. DI Joyce's comment on the statement is interesting, 'considering Moran's connection with secret societies in Co. Sligo, would go far to convince a Sligo jury of Muldowney's complicity in the crime, as it shows that he was a sworn Fenian before he joined the Force. I am aware that it is difficult to convince most people that a policeman would mix himself up in such a crime, but this evidence would throw a new light upon it'. Joyce concluded by stating that 'Moran is a most intelligent class of witness, and he says that the other prisoners are becoming afraid of Muldowney giving evidence against them, and if the latter were, in due course, furnished with a copy of Moran's evidence it might produce a good effect'.[71]

The accounts given by Gavin and Moran paint a vivid picture of the atmosphere of suspicion and fear that surrounded prisoners on remand, with prisoners keeping a close watch on fellow inmates going to the governor's office to be interviewed by lawyers and police. There was a constant fear that their colleagues would elect to give evidence against them to save their own lives and gain financial reward. Gavin and Moran were prime examples of participants in crimes who became approvers. The fact that both men were serial informers probably indicates their desire to further ingratiate themselves with the authorities in the hope of improving their monetary rewards. Gavin was a young man who was keen to emigrate and start a new life, but his traitorous behaviour meant that the whole family had to leave the country for fear of retribution by their neighbours. Moran's mother also became a victim, an unfortunate widow with three young children, one of them 'a cripple and bedridden'.[72] She owned a public house and a small farm but became destitute after her son gave evidence because no one would enter the public house. The crown increased her support to £2 per week from August 1884 on the recommendation of Captain A.S. Butler DM. In his opinion,

> nothing is more certain to destroy our utility in the detection of crime than a system of false economy in payment of witnesses and those from whom information is to be had; if these men are not satisfied our efforts are paralyzed and the result will be a certain increase of crime and a very much larger bill in consequence.[73]

Moran was a busy man during the summer of 1884. He was staying in the crown witness depot in Clontarf and travelled to Sligo for the assizes in June. In

71 NAI CSO RP 1884/15544 in 1885/5161, Joyce to Anderson, 29 June 1884. 72 NAI CSO RP 1884/11687, report of DI Phillips, Tubbercurry, 9 May 1884. 73 NAI CSO RP 1885/815, Butler to Anderson, 15 Aug. 1884.

July, he went to Birmingham to give information regarding John Daly.[74] He returned to Warwick assizes for the trial of Daly, who was charged with treason felony for receiving a quantity of explosives. Daly conducted his own defence and became incensed when Moran appeared as a witness. Moran admitted to being an informer and he claimed to have seen Daly in Tubbercurry on five or six occasions and said he had been told that Daly was a Fenian organizer. The judge, addressing the jury, said that Moran acknowledged that he was infamous and Daly referred to him shivering and trembling in court, 'a diabolical and self-admitted conspirator'.[75] Daly was found guilty and sentenced to life imprisonment; although it was widely believed that the police trapped him into receiving the parcels of explosives.[76]

Moran returned to Sligo and was present for Finnegan's second trial, but was not called to give evidence. The trial of P.N. Fitzgerald, charged with treason felony, resumed at the Dublin Commission on 7 November 1884.[77] The charge that Fitzgerald was a Fenian depended on the evidence of Patrick Delaney and John Moran. Delaney had been sentenced to death for participation in the Phoenix Park murders and was already serving a sentence of fifteen years for the attack on Judge Lawson. Judge Harrison described Moran's evidence as a tangled mess and the defence counsel pointed out five discrepancies with his original statement.[78] Addressing the jury, Judge Harrison said 'The discrepancies in Moran's evidence had been pointed out; the witness' character had been pointed out, and it would be for them to say whether a man of that character was one to whose evidence they would attach credence'.[79] Fitzgerald was acquitted on a lesser charge of conspiracy to murder and the remaining twelve prisoners were released. After the trial, discussions took place regarding the disposal of Moran. DI Heard, who was in charge of crown witnesses, stated that it would be very desirable to settle with him as soon as possible as it would be difficult to provide protection because of bitter feelings towards him.[80] The difficulties about sending anyone 'tainted with crime' were raised by the under secretary, and arrangements were made to send John Moran to San Francisco; he sailed from Londonderry on 5 January 1885. Travel expenses amounted to £22 19s. 6d. An outfit of clothes cost £4 19s. 6d., and Moran was given a cheque for £100.

---

74 John Daly was a Fenian who emigrated to America after the rising of 1867. He returned to Ireland in 1878 and became a member of the supreme council and an organizer for the IRB. 75 *Freeman's Journal*, 2 Aug. 1884. 76 In 1892, John Redmond appealed for amnesty for Daly and quoted Chief Constable Farndale, Birmingham, who stated that the man (Daniel O'Neill) who handed the explosives to Daly was an RIC agent. See J.E. Redmond, quoted in Sean McConville, *Irish political prisoners* (London, 2003), p. 384. See also William O'Brien & Desmond Ryan (eds), *Devoy's post bag* (Dublin, 1948), ii, pp 242–3. Daly was granted amnesty in 1896. 77 *Freeman's Journal*, 8 Nov. 1884. 78 *Freeman's Journal*, 10 Nov. 1884. 79 *Freeman's Journal*, 11 Nov. 1884. 80 NAI CSO RP 1884/19177 in 1885/815.

7 Trial by jury and the course of justice

During the Land War, widespread agitation resulted in a marked increase in what were termed 'agrarian offences'. The majority concerned intimidation by word of mouth or by threatening letters and boycotting, but in addition there was an increase of firing into houses, wounding of persons and animals, and homicide. The detection and conviction rates of those responsible for these offences were very low because of the communal solidarity and the fear of retaliation that protected the perpetrators. The ability to change the venue of trials and the use of special juries ensured that the predominantly Catholic defendants were tried before Protestant jurors of a different social class. Throughout the nineteenth century, controversy surrounded trial by jury in Ireland. Among the measures adopted to reform the system were the Jury Acts of 1871 and 1876, and a select committee on Irish Jury Laws reported in August 1881.[1] Already provided in the 1871 act were powers to establish lists of special jurors with a higher rateable qualification than common jurors, and authority was conferred on the attorney general to change the venues of trials to venues outside the locality in which crimes had been committed. This power had been used rarely before the enactment of the Prevention of Crime (Ireland) Act of 1882. The select committee included in its membership a number of prominent Irish landlords, including the marquess of Landsdowne, Lord Inchiquin, Lord Emly and Lord Ardilaun. The witnesses examined were drawn from RMs, including RMs Clifford Lloyd and Henry Arthur Blake, CS George Bolton, Justices Barry, Fitzgerald (later Lord Fitzgerald) and James Lawson, and other prominent lawyers. The report of the committee commented: 'From some parts of the country, strong testimony has been borne to the integrity and intelligence with which juries have acted'. They found much cause for complaint, 'in places where that agitation is most deeply seated, the law has been again and again violated with impunity, because of the difficulty of obtaining evidence and because jurors refused to find verdicts in accordance with the facts'. In evidence to the committee, RM Henry Arthur Blake, Tuam (later appointed SRM for Galway), referred to the fact that there was 'no feeling whatever of reverence for the law, and in cases where there is a prevailing public sentiment in either political or agrarian cases, it is very difficult to obtain convictions'. A year later, Blake even expressed the opinion that 'he could not trust a jury of RMs at the moment'.[2]

The select committee made a number of recommendations, including enforcement of fines for non-attendance of jurors and extension of the qualifications for

---

1 Select committee of the House of Lords appointed to inquire into the operation of the Irish jury laws.   2 BL Spencer papers, 76854, Spencer to Gladstone, 8 May 1882.

jury service to allow retired army officers, graduates of universities and other persons of 'education, position or antecedents' to serve on juries. The challenging of jurors was addressed by the recommendation that, while the crown should continue to have an unlimited right of challenge, the defendant's right should be reduced from twenty challenges to six, and that, in the case of special juries, 'the right of challenge should no longer be conceded'. Clearly, these recommendations would ensure that the crown had even greater control over the selection of juries than before. Finally, it was suggested that 'it will be for Her Majesty's government to determine whether trial by jury should for a limited time, within a limited area, and in regard to crimes of a well-defined character, be replaced by some form of trial less liable to abuse'. This recommendation was indeed included in the Prevention of Crime (Ireland) Act the following year, but, because of objections by the Irish judges, it was not implemented.

Nationalists, however, had a different perception of what constituted impartial juries and honest verdicts in the courts and they particularly entertained grave reservations regarding jury selection. McEldowney quotes from the memorandum of Constantine Molloy, an Irish lawyer:

> That this privilege for the crown to stand by jurors has been sometime abused there can be no question, and thereby convictions obtained in cases where this right has been abused have lost all that moral weight which is so essentially necessary to give due effect to the administration of the law.[3]

In 1887, Lord Fitzgerald explained that the phrase 'jury packing' had a particular meaning in Ireland: 'By jury packing was popularly meant the exclusion of Roman Catholics who were returned on the panel from taking part in trials'.[4] It was widely believed that police officers scrutinized jury panels and identified on the one hand individuals involved in the Land League and on the other members of the gentry and the middle and upper classes. The possession of obvious English or Irish surnames was also a criterion for challenge by either the prosecution or defence solicitors.[5]

The abuse was indeed institutionalized and accepted as a necessary fact of life by the chief secretary, W.E. Forster. In a letter to Prime Minister Gladstone, prior to the introduction of the Prevention of Crime (Ireland) Act, he proposed a

> vigorous and determined effort to secure convictions of men notoriously guilty. For this purpose, I do not think amendment of the jury laws will

3 HC 1873 (283), xv, appendix 4. Select committee on juries (Ireland), quoted in John F. McEldowney, 'Some aspects of law and policy in the administration of criminal justice in nineteenth-century Ireland' in McEldowney & O'Higgins, *The common law tradition: essays in Irish legal history* (Dublin, 1990), pp 117–55. 4 Ibid. 5 Ball, *Policing the Land War*, ch. 9.

suffice. We cannot return to the old system of packing juries and tinkering; such a bitter system of challenging etc., may be an improvement, but no cure for the present evil. I think we cannot stop short of taking temporary powers to try agrarian offences, without jury, by special legal commissioners.

He was uncertain if this draconian measure should be used only in disturbed areas 'notorious for jury failure' or in cases 'in which the judge reports after trial that the verdict is against evidence'.[6] So, the blatantly illegal tactic of jury packing was to be supplanted by another mechanism more likely to deliver the 'right' verdicts. That Gladstone was well aware of the practice is evident from his comment when Peter O'Brien became lord chief justice in 1889: 'The AG has been rewarded for his jury packing in Ireland'. For a number of years prior to that, O'Brien was popularly known as 'Peter the Packer'.

Following the introduction of the Prevention of Crime (Ireland) Act of 1882, attempts were made to improve the conviction rate, particularly in counties that were considered impossible, such as Galway.[7] The attorney general made much greater use of his power to change the venue of trials to venues outside the area in which the crime was committed. Shortly after the act became law, the Dublin Commission was set up to try cases from elsewhere in the country and, in order to improve the chances of obtaining convictions, the Dublin city and county panels were amalgamated to dilute the influence of jurors drawn from the farming class. Several trials, including the Maamtrasna case, were transferred to Dublin, and the desired guilty verdicts were obtained. The Cork jury panels were also manipulated by amalgamating the city and county panels, which produced juries with much fewer representatives of the farming class and a greater proportion of landed gentry, merchants and professional people.[8] Sligo was another popular choice for trials because of the expectation that 'suitable' jurors would be available for selection. There was an increased referral rate to the winter assizes that heard cases from several counties, thus avoiding the possible bias of local juries and, as a result, the Sligo winter assizes enjoyed a significantly higher rate of convictions.[9] To compensate for the additional costs of witnesses attending distant venues, the act allowed for the payment of their expenses.

The act made provision for the payment of the fees of defence counsel and this probably contributed to the achievement of acquittals in some cases. However, it was the subject of criticism in parliament because generally the more powerful leading counsel was employed for the prosecution and the less able counsel assigned to the defence. Local communities were also aware of this

6 Thomas Wemyss Reid, *Life of the Rt Hon. W.E. Forster* (New York, 1970), ii, p. 417, Forster to Gladstone, 7 Apr. 1882. 7 NAI CSO RP 1891/28047, memorandum of John Naish. 8 Ball, *Policing the Land War*, p. 345. 9 NAI CSO RP 1883/2142, verdicts in crimes act trials.

disparity and often raised funds by public collection to employ better counsel to defend cases.[10]

Allegations of irregularities in jury selection by the authorities were widespread and the detailed analysis by Stephen Ball of cases tried at the Dublin Commission demonstrates the extent of the manipulation of jury selection.[11] It was believed that the police and sheriff knew the religion of jurors and that this knowledge was used by the crown solicitor to produce juries that were disposed to bring in guilty verdicts. Ball calculated that of the two hundred jurors on the panel, eighty-five (42 per cent) were Catholic but only thirty-four jurors (17 per cent) who deliberated in the nine agrarian trials were Catholic. In the seven most serious cases, only 9 per cent of the jurors were Catholic. In the capital cases, the juries were entirely composed of Protestants, all of the Catholic jurors being ordered to stand aside.[12] In a letter to Horace Seymour,[13] Spencer expressed his concerns:

> I am very much annoyed at the look of the jury question in Dublin. I have no reason to doubt the honesty of the attorney and solicitor general's assurances and directions that no religious objections should be made to jurors, but the case looks very much against us on paper.[14]

Jury packing was also evident in the trials of Muldowney and Finnegan at the Sligo assizes. In the case of Muldowney, the jury at the first trial was drawn largely from the landed gentry of Sligo, and in the second trial there were ten Protestants and two Catholics on the jury. At the trials of Finnegan, the juries were composed entirely of Protestants. At the second trial, a man called Robert Porteous, who had been a jury member at Muldowney's second trial, was called to serve. He wished to be excused, saying that he had made up his mind about the verdict before Finnegan's trial started. However, the attorney general insisted that he be empanelled. These matters received much publicity in the local, but not in the national, press and neither were they mentioned during the parliamentary debates on the Maamtrasna case.

Shortly after Thomas Casey's public confession of perjury during the Maamtrasna trials, Timothy Harrington MP asked a question in the House of Commons on 11 August about the revelations, and was assured by Lord Hartington, the home secretary, that an enquiry would be made into the matter. Harrington demanded a full public enquiry and his motion before the House of Commons on 24 October proposed that the administration of the Prevention of

---

10 Cf. employment of Dr Webb QC in Finnegan's second trial (see above, p. 67). 11 Ball, *Policing the Land War*, ch. 9. 12 These included the Maamtrasna, Letterfrack and Clonbur trials. 13 Horace Seymour (1843–1902), permanent secretary of the treasury and chancellor of the exchequer. 14 Gordon, *The Red Earl*, Lord Spencer to Horace Seymour, 29 Oct. 1882, 286, pp 224–5.

Crime (Ireland) Act had led to the execution of Myles Joyce and sentences of life imprisonment for four other innocent men. In his response, the home secretary, Sir William Harcourt, argued that if the inquiry was allowed it would make Spencer's position untenable and 'would be fatal to the administration of the crown in Ireland'. The motion was defeated by 219 votes to forty-eight. Spencer concluded that the verdict and the sentence were right and just.[15]

The correctness of verdicts was again a matter for debate in the House of Commons in July 1885, when Charles Stewart Parnell tabled a motion: 'That in the opinion of this house, it is the duty of the government to institute strict inquiry into the evidence and convictions in the Maamtrasna, Barbavilla, Crossmaglen and Castleisland cases'.[16] These were cases in which witnesses at the trials had subsequently declared that they had committed perjury. In relation to the Castleisland case and the execution of two men, Sylvester Poff and James Barrett on 23 January 1883, Chief Secretary Trevelyan's initial reaction was recorded in a letter to Spencer: 'I see a madman has claimed to be the murderer in the case'.[17] The second trial of Finnegan was not mentioned in the several debates in parliament even though Dr T.E. Webb QC had clearly demonstrated that perjury had been committed in that case as well.

At the winter assizes of 1886, presided over by the Lord Chief Baron, Christopher Palles,[18] the spotlight was cast upon Sligo and its juries. The cases for trial were those of thirty-six men arrested in Woodford, Co. Galway, on 27 August 1886. The arrests followed the 'Siege of Saunders Fort',[19] which involved a confrontation between a group of men resisting the eviction of Thomas Saunders and two hundred military, two hundred police and bailiffs.

The first jury selected was composed of ten Protestants and two Catholics, one of whom was a landlord and the other a bailiff. The second jury was composed of twelve Protestants and on the third there was a single Catholic. Three grave breaches of Lord O'Hagan's rules for the selection of juries were exposed and as a result, despite strenuous objections from the crown counsel, Sergeant Peter O'Brien, Chief Baron Palles quashed the jury panel. The reconstituted panel and the juries selected from it (see table 3, p. 100) were also unbalanced, with a large majority of Protestants on each one in a county where Catholics outnumbered Protestants by nine to one.[20] The crown was able to achieve this outcome because it was allowed to challenge far more jurors than the six challenges allowed to the defence. The crown also attempted to have jurors sworn in who had already returned guilty verdicts at earlier trials. This request

15 For an extended account of the controversy, see Waldron, *Maamtrasna*, chs 14 and 15, pp 232–99. 16 *Freeman's Journal*, 15 July 1885. 17 BL Spencer papers, 76965, Trevelyan to Spencer, 15 Aug. 1884. 18 Christopher Palles (1831–1920), attorney general 1873, retired on fall of ministry 1874; returned as MP for Londonderry in same year; AG again in 1880 and re-elected MP in same year, chancellor in 1881; chief baron in 1886. 19 Thomas Saunders was a tenant of Lord Clanrickarde under threat of eviction for non-payment of rent. 20 *Irish Times*, 8 & 14 Dec. 1886, *Tuam News*, 10 Dec. 1886, *Pall Mall Gazette*, 10 Dec. 1886.

Table 3 Composition of juries during the Sligo winter assizes, 1886 (cited in John J. Clancy MP, *Six months of 'Unionist' rule* (London, 1887), p. 51).

	Challenged by crown		Defence	Juries constituted	
	Catholics	*Protestants*		*Catholics*	*Protestants*
Jury 1	12	5	6	2	10
Jury 2	12	0	6	0	12
Jury 3	25	5	6	1	11
Jury 4	9	0	6	3	9
Jury 5	9	3	6	0	12
Jury 6	16	0	6	6	6
Totals	83	13	36	12	60

was disallowed by the chief baron, but in fact five jurors acted in more than one of the trials and three acted in three trials.

The prisoners were committed on a charge of felony and were therefore not granted bail. They remained in custody until the trial commenced, at which time the charge of felony was dropped. On 21 December 1886, ten of the accused were tried and the jury repeatedly returned to the court to state that they could not agree a verdict. The chief baron essentially coerced the jury to retire each time and finally the judge directed the jury to return a guilty verdict on a count of wilful obstruction of the sheriff. A total of thirty-six prisoners were tried and convicted. Thirty-one of those were given periods of imprisonment of between twelve and eighteen months, while five were discharged on bail.[21] One of those imprisoned, a 23-year-old man, Tommy Larkin of Gurteeny, Woodford, died in Kilkenny Jail on 27 September 1887 following a brief illness.

During the trials, there was adverse press comment and the *Tuam News* referred to the cloud of suspicion over the town of Sligo and 'the whole rotten system of government by jury packing'.[22] The procedures and outcome of the trials were a source of considerable public disquiet and three petitions were submitted to Dublin Castle after the assizes. The first was signed by three bishops and fifty-three priests from local dioceses and the second by ninety-nine Catholic jurors empanelled for the assizes who protested against 1) the illegal manner in which Lord O'Hagan's 1876 Jury Act was violated; 2) the deliberate and systematic exclusion of Catholics from juries; and 3) the hardship on them (the jurors) to attend for several weeks in order to be insulted by not being selected. They declared that

> the object and aim of the crown officials in their selection of jurors and
> manipulation of jury lists was the conviction of the prisoners and that

21 *Irish Times*, 22 Dec. 1886; *Freeman's Journal*, 6 Jan. 1887.   22 *Tuam News*, 10 Dec. 1886.

they were set aside for no other reason than there was no hope to cajole or persuade, much less coerce them to bring in verdicts of guilty where they saw no guilt. Such misconduct of crown officers authorized and directed by the crown itself is a monstrous evil and scandal. We pray our representatives in parliament to take the earliest opportunity of calling the attentions of parliament to these hateful evils of jury packing; and we feel confident that every lover of justice and social order in the House of Commons will unite with them to obtain the needful amendment of the jury laws, and the restriction of the abused and unjust privileges.

An indication of the extent of the disquiet can be appreciated from the third petition, signed by fifty-one non-Catholic jurors, stating that

we wish to express for ourselves the dissatisfaction with which we have witnessed, not only during the last assizes, but at the ordinary assizes and quarter sessions of our county, the systematic exclusion of Catholics from the trials of cases in which the crown was anxious to obtain convictions ... such methods bring the law into contempt and give rise to social discord between Irishmen of different creeds.[23]

In the trial of John Dillon, Matthew Harris, David Sheehy, Daniel Crilly and William O'Brien, who were arrested in Loughrea during the second phase of the Plan of Campaign (the second phase of the Land War, 1886–91), similar irregularities of jury selection were exposed. The selection of the jury panel was carried out illegally, and instead of having one hundred Protestants and 150 Catholics, it comprised 150 Protestants and one hundred Catholics. There was a systematic exclusion of jurors bearing what appeared to be Catholic names, and the crown, exercising its right to order jurors to 'stand by', achieved their aim of packing the jury with nine Protestants and three Catholics. Despite the packing of the jury, a verdict of acquittal was returned. In a pamphlet published after the trial, Daniel Crilly, one of the accused, stated that

Trial by jury for political and quasi-political offences has been ever more or less of a make-believe and pretence in Ireland. Down to the present time, the crown has succeeded in asserting the law of the land by such an arrangement of the jury system as, in political trials, would secure the presence of men upon whom the crown officers could rely.[24]

Judge James Murphy refused to quash the illegal jury panel. This should come as no surprise, because he also presided over the packing of the juries at the trials of Muldowney and Finnegan (see above, chs 4, 5).

23 John J. Clancy, *Six months of 'Unionist' rule* (1887); E.P.S. Counsel, *Jury packing* (Dublin, 1887). **24** Daniel Crilly, *Jury packing in Ireland* (Dublin, 1887).

Can there be any surprise that the nationalist community felt alienated from the law in the light of the flagrant abuse of the Jury Act, which was specifically enacted to regularize procedures in jury selection? The juries at the Dublin Commission and elsewhere certainly performed as Forster and the establishment desired, but the practise of jury manipulation inevitably brought the law into disrepute. Speaking in the House of Lords in 1908, the lord chancellor, Lord Loreburn, stated that

> Packing juries was one of the methods by which alone, a government determined to depart from the ordinary law and determined to govern against the sympathies of the people, could govern Ireland. Packing juries was sure to bring about injustice.[25]

In the case of the Craughwell prisoners, an unjust verdict was achieved and the injustice blighted the victims' lives throughout their long sojourns in prison.

25 R. Barry O'Brien, *Dublin Castle and the Irish people* (London, 1912), p. 134.

8 The Craughwell prisoners' life in jail

Michael Muldowney was transferred from Galway Jail to Mountjoy Prison in Dublin on 15 August 1884, and Patrick Finnegan followed on 28 August. When Finnegan was *en route* to Dublin, a large crowd gathered at Athenry station and it was there that he met his father and mother for the last time, because neither visited him in prison and they died several years before his release. On the arrival of the prisoners in Mountjoy, the Penal Record document[1] was completed with the usual personal details, and measurements of height and weight and any distinctive marks were recorded.

The Craughwell prisoners' experience of prison began with a period of solitary confinement lasting nine months, the standard duration for penal servitude at that time. In the wards there were three tiers of cells, each measuring seven feet by fourteen feet and ten feet high.[2] The furniture consisted of a table, stool and a plank bed with blankets that were changed yearly. In one corner, there were two small shelves holding two enamelled pint tins, a tin plate and, on the upper shelf, a Bible, a prayer book and a piece of soap. The prisoners learned to cope with the dreary prison food that consisted mainly of bread and cocoa or milk. After his release, Finnegan frequently commented on the monotony of the food and the insufficient rations and he hated to see food wasted in the home. The prison photographs record the ageing effect of the diet and the confinement on both prisoners and, in Finnegan's case, subsequent photographs show a marked improvement of his appearance (fig. 10, p. 104). Despite the monotony of the diet both prisoners gained weight during their confinement, in the case of Muldowney a total of twenty pounds.

In the earlier part of the century, infectious diseases such as cholera were common in prisons, but conditions had improved by the 1880s and there was a strong emphasis on cleanliness, with regular washing out of cells, landings and stairs. Pots were put into the cells and earth closets were placed in the hall.[3]

Finnegan's medical record is quite brief, with minor infections and injuries such as a sprained ankle and an incised wound of the hand. An abscess on the hip was lanced in 1890 and an alveolar abscess due to a dental infection was treated in the same year. Muldowney also remained healthy throughout his prison sentence, with only trivial medical complaints recorded.

1 The information regarding the prisoners' experiences of prison life, petitions etc. is contained in NAI CRF misc. 1903/484. 2 Details of accommodation and conditions are contained in Sean Milroy, *Memories of Mountjoy* (London, Dublin, 1917). 3 Tim Carey, *Mountjoy: the story of a prison* (Cork, 2000), p. 90.

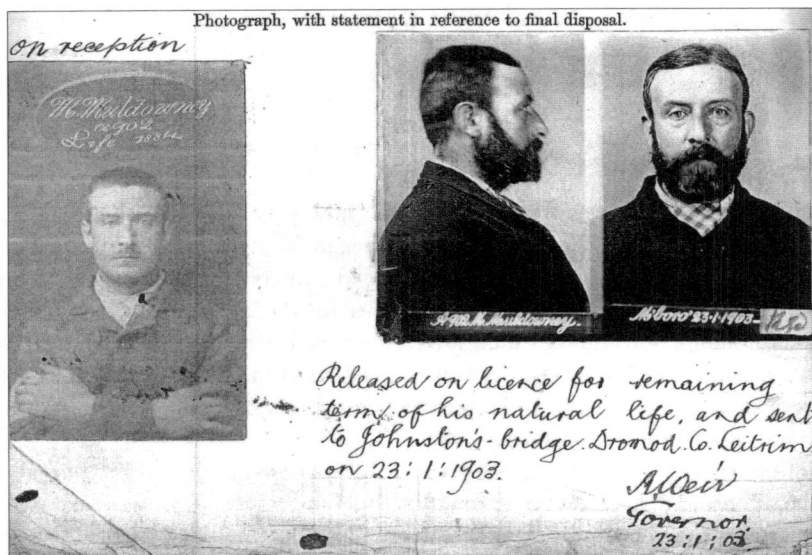

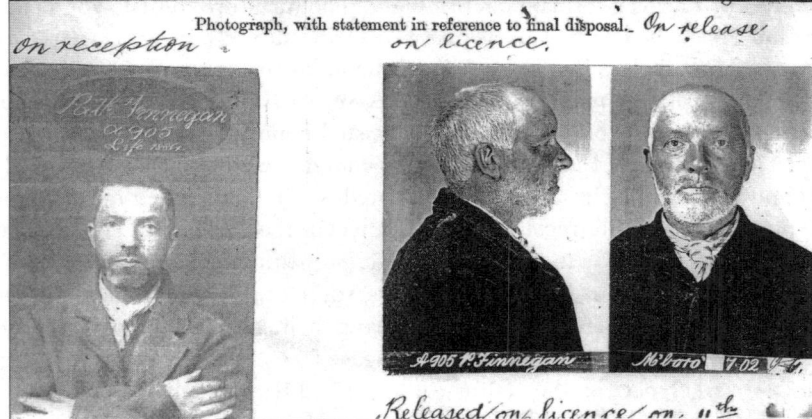

10 Photographs of prisoners Muldowney (*above*) and Finnegan (*below*) on reception into prison (*left*) and again on release (*right*) (National Archives of Ireland Convict Reference File, Miscellaneous 1903; image reproduced courtesy of the Director of the National Archives of Ireland).

The prisoners' lives were carefully organized by means of rules and regulations and infringement resulted in punishments of varying severity. Their daily routine was strictly regimented, with a wake-up call by the jangling triangles at 6am, breakfast at 8am and work until the midday meal at 12.45pm. Work occupied the afternoon until a return to the cells at 5pm. Sean Milroy, who was an inmate in the early years of the twentieth century, described the night as a time of 'loneliness, solitude and silence', except for the noise of a tram on the North Circular Road and the occasional hoot of a railway engine.[4] Exercise took place on Sundays and lasted for two hours. The exercise area consisted of three concentric rings occupied by prisoners according to their exercise capacities, with the weakest walking in the inner ring. A certain distance separated the prisoners but they were able to hold surreptitious conversations with their neighbours.

It is a testament to the prisoners' equable temperaments that there were very few reprimands for prison offences. In May 1887, Finnegan was cautioned for breaking prison rules and, in June 1895, 'for speaking in an insolent manner when before the governor'. As a result, he was not allowed to work outside the prison again without special sanction. In like manner, there was only one reprimand recorded in Muldowney's file. Finnegan later referred to his surprise at seeing a number of men attending mass who were chained hand and foot. A whispered enquiry to another prisoner, P.W. Nally, from Balla, Co. Mayo, elicited the explanation that it was part of the punishment regime for serious infraction of prison rules.

Initially, both prisoners were engaged in picking oakum, that most tedious of occupations in which old ropes were unpicked and the loose fibre was then used for caulking ships' seams and other purposes. This practice was phased out in the latter part of the nineteenth century. Work in the 'stickyard' involved the splitting of logs and binding them into bundles. Muldowney was chiefly engaged in work as a carpenter and storeman, while Finnegan worked as a labourer, carpenter and wardsman and was also engaged in the making of mats. Payments for work done were recorded on special forms and typically a sum of 5s. was earned in six months. Prisoners attended the prison school for six hours weekly and Finnegan benefited greatly from this, showing a marked improvement in language and writing skills.

There were strict limits on the number of visits and letters the prisoners could send and receive. The general rule allowed one letter during the first week after sentence and subsequently at intervals of two to six months, according to their designated class. Misconduct could result in the withdrawal of the privilege for a time. All letters were read by the governor and chaplain and the purpose of communicating was defined as 'enabling prisoners to keep up a connection with their respectable friends' and 'not that they may hear the news of the day'.[5] Infringement of the rules could lead to the suppression of letters and this happened to both Craughwell prisoners on several occasions.

Finnegan sent between three and five letters annually and received from one to four; in the early years all communications were exchanged with his father. Muldowney was subjected to a more restricted regime; exceptionally, he was

4 Milroy, *Memories of Mountjoy*, p. 78.   5 NAI CRF misc. 1903/484.

allowed to send four letters in 1897 but he was usually restricted to sending one or two letters and he never received more than two per year. The first exchange of letters was with his father but thereafter his principal correspondent was his uncle Michael. In terms of visits, Finnegan had three visits in 1885, 1887, 1889 and 1897, and otherwise the number of visits varied between none and two per year. Muldowney was again treated more rigidly; he received four visits in 1885 and thereafter between none and two per year. It seems likely that the harsh treatment was deliberate and dictated by a perception that he had disgraced his calling as a policeman. For instance, in October 1885, Muldowney's uncle, Michael Mahon, requested a visit by himself and Muldowney's sister, Ellen. The letter was sent to the chairman of the General Prisons Board, who decided that the visit could go ahead but it would have to be *in lieu* of Muldowney's next due visit in 1886. As a result, he did not receive another visit until September 1886.

PETITIONS FOR RELEASE

Petitions for release could be sent to the lord lieutenant at any time after sentence and the first petition on behalf of Muldowney was prepared by his solicitor, Richard Jennings, and submitted in October 1885 to Lord Carnarvon.[6] A letter of support from Lord Granard accompanied it. The petition outlined a detailed defence of Muldowney's record as a policeman, and his loyalty to the queen. It also criticized the admissibility of statements that were made by him during the investigations before he was cautioned that he was suspected of a crime. It stated that if Muldowney were guilty of the crime he would not have returned to Galway when recalled and could have taken the easy option of going to Queenstown and emigrating to America. Jennings identified the many contradictory statements of the two informers – Raftery and Moran – and provided a detailed refutation of their evidence. He also drew attention to the abandonment of the trials of the other prisoners in March 1885, stating that

> the attorney general and the crown counsel, by thus consenting to enter a *nolle prosequi* in cases of such moment and magnitude, must, consistently with their clear and obvious duty to the public, have felt that the evidence was unreliable, and that the liberty of the accused should not have been imperilled on untrustworthy accusations. This being so, such a view presses with greater force in the case of Muldowney, who was *prima facie* less likely to engage in agrarian outrages, whose character was high in the police force, and who was one of the most unlikely men for

6 Henry, Earl of Carnarvon succeeded Spencer as lord lieutenant in June 1885.

conspirators to resort to for aid, in the perpetration of a barbarous midnight murder.

The petition and files were sent to the Rt Hon. Dr J.T. Ball,[7] who expressed the opinion that

> The question of credibility of Moran and Raftery was essentially for the jury as only those who heard them could estimate their intelligence or truthfulness as to whether they told what they saw or did they invent the statements.[8]

He referred to the evidence of Mary Forde and Margaret Raftery that placed Muldowney and Raftery in different places and contradicted Raftery's evidence. Ball considered that some statements by Muldowney were untrue and led to a conclusion of some sort of participation. Ball suggested that the lord lieutenant should speak to Judge Murphy regarding the reasons for the commutation that 'may be of a character either to fortify or preclude further interference'. However, there is no indication in the files that Murphy's opinion was sought at that time. In fact, the under secretary, Dr Kaye, advised referral to the lord chancellor before seeking Murphy's opinion. In reply, Lord Ashbourne[9] commented on the unequivocal report of the judge that the evidence against the prisoner was 'clear and conclusive' and advised that the 'the law should take its course', a decision endorsed by the initial of Lord Carnarvon on 27 October 1885. The damning phrase of Judge Murphy – clear and conclusive – was thus identified as the most important judgment in the case and was to return again and again in response to petitions from both prisoners leading to the regular and increasingly perfunctory rejection of all appeals. The comment was frequently linked with the forthright conclusion that 'the law must take its course'.

A petition on behalf of both prisoners was presented to the new lord lieutenant[10] in February 1886. Clergymen from the local parishes, including the parish priests of Craughwell, Ardrahan, Clarinbridge and Ballinderecen, signed it. They stated that after mature consideration, they had reason to believe that the prisoners were innocent and referred to events at the trials and the characters of the prosecution witnesses. A judicial review was carried out by the chief baron, Richard Dowse, who stated that

7 John Thomas Ball (1815–98) was a graduate of TCD, Doctor of Laws 1844, QC 1853, solicitor general and attorney general in Disraeli's first administration until 1868; MP 1868–75; AG 1874, lord chancellor 1875, author of *Historical review of the legislative systems operative in Ireland* (1888). 8 NAI CRF misc. 1903/484. 9 Edward Gibson, Lord Ashbourne (1837–1913), graduate of TCD, QC 1872, AG 1877–80, lord chancellor 1885–6, 1895–1905. 10 John Campbell Gordon, 1st marquis of Aberdeen (1847–1934), appointed lord lieutenant in Feb. 1886 and again in 1905 (to 1915).

> I see no grounds for any inquiry into the facts, there may be cases in
> which an inquiry meets the need of justice. I do not think this is one of
> them. No further action can be taken and above all no reason is shown
> for any further action.[11]

There was an obvious reluctance on the part of the crown to reopen a case they
considered closed. The decision of Dowse was not based on a transcript of
evidence and heavy reliance was placed on the depositions and the reports of
Judge Murphy. Therefore, all of the reviews of the case were based on partial
accounts of the proceedings in court. Michael Mahon, Muldowney's uncle,
pursued the issue again in May 1886, submitting on his own behalf the petition
previously submitted by Richard Jennings; it promptly received the usual rejection.

In May 1888, Finnegan appealed on his own account and referred to the
evidence placing him in Cawley's public house at the time of the murder. He had
also become aware of the controversy regarding jury packing at the Sligo assizes
in 1886 and the quashing of the jury panel. He referred to the offer that
emanated from the crown counsel and communicated to him by his defence
counsel, George Orme Malley, that a sentence of ten years imprisonment would
be imposed if he pleaded guilty to a charge of conspiracy to murder. He had
declined the offer because he was innocent. The petition was submitted on 18
May and the decision of the lord lieutenant was issued one week later.[12] The
response was inevitably: 'the law must take its course'.

Almost three years elapsed before the next petition was sent to Arthur James
Balfour, the chief secretary, by Lieutenant Colonel John Nolan, MP for Galway.
He asked Balfour to 'draw the attention of the lord lieutenant[13] to the character
of the signatures to the memorial as the gentlemen who have signed include
every class of opinion and politics'. The petition is of particular importance
because it was signed by a number of clergymen and twenty landlords and
justices of the peace, who would not have harboured much sympathy for the
nationalist cause. They wished to inform Lord Zetland that 'the unanimous
public opinion is very strongly in favour of the innocence of Finnegan and
believed him to be guiltless of the crime'. Attention was drawn to the release of
the four remaining prisoners faced with the same evidence in 1885 and a special
plea was made on behalf of Finnegan's elderly parents. Included among the
signatures were those of Isidore Bourke, who had succeeded the assassinated
Walter Bourke and had dismissed the informer Raftery, Burton Persse (from
Moyode), who had also dismissed Raftery, Dudley Persse (Roxborough), the
father of Lady Gregory, Edward Martyn (Tullira), J.D. Daly (Castledaly), John

11 Richard Dowse (1824–90), QC 1863, MP for Londonderry 1868, solicitor general 1870, AG
and baron of the exchequer 1872.   12 Charles Stewart, marquis of Londonderry, became lord
lieutenant on 5 Aug. 1886.   13 Laurence Dundas, earl of Zetland, lord lieutenant 1889–1902.

W. Lambert (Aggard) and Walter P. Lambert (Castle Ellen). In addition, the parish priests and curates of all the local parishes signed the petition. The signatories of this powerful appeal would have expected that it would be given careful attention, but instead only five days were required for the customary rejection to be issued by Lord Zetland: 'the law must take its course'.

The rejection of the very detailed submissions on behalf of Muldowney in 1886 and the submission on behalf of both prisoners in 1888 clearly acted as a discouragement to appeals because there was a lapse of four years until April 1892 when Lieutenant Colonel Nolan asked the chief secretary a question in parliament regarding the Craughwell prisoners.[14] The reply merely informed Nolan that both prisoners were still in custody. In October 1893, Muldowney's uncle, Michael Mahon, again submitted a petition, accompanied by a letter from the bishop of Ardagh and Clonmacnoise. The petition was referred to Samuel Walker,[15] the lord chancellor, for his opinion and he replied to the chief secretary, John Morley, on 21 November 1893. His response, if transmitted to the petitioner, would have only deepened the sense of despondency regarding a pardon:

> In this case, there is no new ground suggested throwing doubt upon the evidence given at the trial. That being so, I think the case should be considered on the hypothesis that the verdict was right. The report of the learned judge states that the evidence was clear and conclusive. I cannot think that at the end of nine years there is any ground for interfering. The convict is an ex-constable who was on protection duty – a position of trust – and betrayed it and joined the secret societies of the district. To institute an inquiry would manifestly be unprecedented and dangerous. It was already refused on the fullest consideration (see Baron Dowse's minute of 19 February 1886). I cannot think that there is any ground for exercising the clemency of the crown.[16]

In this instance, the danger of exposing the law to enquiry and the additional disgrace of Muldowney's 'betrayal' are the prominent features.

In April 1894, Finnegan appealed again to the lord lieutenant,[17] and on this occasion he wrote the petition himself. He referred to the fact that he was now in jail for eleven years and three months from the date of his arrest. He stated that he was not present at the murder and that the 'two wretched men', Moran and Raftery, did not 'swear one word of truth' against him and that they did it for the sake of the £200 reward offered by the crown. He commented on

14 William Lawies Jackson, created 1st lord Allerton in 1902. 15 Samuel Walker (1832–1911), QC 1872, solicitor general 1883, MP for Co. Londonderry 1884, AG 1885, 1886, lord chancellor, 1892–5 and in 1905 became a baronet in 1906. 16 NAI CRF misc. 1903/484. 17 Robert, Baron Houghton, afterwards Earl of Crewe.

Sergeant Redington and others trying to hire witnesses to swear against him. He pleaded abjectly for mercy but once again his plea was to no avail.

A year later, Finnegan wrote to McDonnell Bodkin who was now an MP.[18] Finnegan addressed him as 'My Dear Counsel' and reminded him that he was a former client of his in 1884. In his letter, Finnegan concentrated on the plea of *nolle prosequi* entered on behalf of the crown in 1885 in relation to Fogarty and the other prisoners who were indicted on the same evidence. He reminded McDonnell Bodkin that the crown had offered all the prisoners a sentence of ten years penal servitude if they pleaded guilty. He informed McDonnell Bodkin that he had now spent twelve years and two months 'unjustly consigned to prison'. He also stated that, if John Morley, now the chief secretary, 'who is a lover of justice, knew the great grievance and injustice that I am so long suffering under … he would in his goodness bring my misery to an end'. He concluded by imploring McDonnell Bodkin to help him: 'Oh, think for a moment how dreadful it is to be years upon years unjustly condemned'. Bodkin wrote to Morley, enclosing the petition and stating: 'I will feel much obliged if you will give as favourable consideration as possible to the enclosed pitiful memorial. I can personally vouch for the substantial accuracy of the statement of facts which it contains'. As well as sending the petition to John Morley, Bodkin asked about the case in the House of Commons on 8 April 1895. The reply prepared for Morley referred to the decisions on previous petitions and dismissed the call for another inquiry. 'As at present advised, there seems to be no sufficient grounds for ordering his release'. Finnegan's confidence in the 'lover of justice' was clearly misplaced. Predictably, the lord lieutenant, Baron Houghton, rejected the petition in the customary manner: 'the law must take its course'.

It is interesting that the briefing for the chief secretary on this occasion was factually inaccurate in many respects. The police in Athenry were asked to supply information about the case and the report of DI Tyrrell contained many inaccuracies and appeared to consist mostly of hearsay; he was also unable to offer any reason for the plea of *nolle prosequi*. This may not be too surprising after a lapse of ten years and the report of DI Alan Bell did not offer any grounds for the decision in March 1885. This highlights the importance of a file issued to Bell immediately before the first trial of Muldowney that was clearly not available for the purpose of DI Tyrrell's report. According to the CSO register for 1884, this file contained information regarding the police investigations of the case. The original request for information for inclusion in the chief secretary's reply came from the Irish office in London, indicating that the file was not available there, nor was it accessible in Dublin Castle; hence the request to the Athenry police office. Recent searches in the National Archives have failed to locate this file, giving rise to the suspicion that it contained material of a very

18 McDonnell Bodkin was elected MP for north Roscommon in 1892, defeating J.J. O'Kelly.

sensitive nature regarding the interaction between the local police and the two informers whose evidence secured the conviction. The last record in the CSO register shows that the file was signed out to DI Alan Bell on the eve of Muldowney's first trial and it is perhaps not surprising that Bell would have wished for concealment if it contained compromising material.[19]

The news of family bereavements was an additional sorrow for the unfortunate prisoners. Finnegan's father had died in 1892, his sister Mary in May 1895 and his brother William in August 1896. The bereavements left his mother in a very poor financial state, but neither the repeated exposure of the faulty evidence nor the straitened family circumstances induced a favourable response to petitions for his release. A sense of desperation was evident in a brief petition that Finnegan submitted on 6 December 1895 in which he recorded that on Christmas Day he would be 99,800 hours under sentence in addition to the nineteen months he had spent in jail before sentence. Only four days were required by the lord lieutenant, Lord Cadogan,[20] to issue the usual response.

In June 1896, Fr Considine, PP of Ardrahan, wrote to David Sheehy, MP for Galway, asking him to intervene in the case. The letter was prompted by comments on the state of Finnegan's health by his brother Tim, following his visit to Mountjoy on 25 April. Fr Considine referred briefly to the main facts relating to the conviction of Finnegan and Muldowney and in particular to the petition signed by twenty magistrates in 1890, asserting Finnegan's innocence. Sheehy wrote to Sir William Ridley MP at the Home Office, stating that 'at the time of Finnegan's conviction a very strong doubt was entertained as to his guilt and that doubt has grown in the minds of the people ever since so much so that the feeling now obtains that the man was absolutely innocent and has suffered those long years for crime [of] which he was not guilty'. He requested that the petition of Lieutenant Colonel Nolan be examined on Finnegan's behalf 'with a view to considering whether true justice does not require that this man's sufferings should cease; that he be released from prison'.[21] The usual verdict quickly arrived on 16 June: 'the law must take its course'. In November of that year, Finnegan submitted another petition and again referred to his long term of imprisonment, which at that stage amounted to thirteen years and eleven months, 'under an error of conviction'. He wrote of his good record in prison, despite 'having to work with prisoners of the most reckless dispositions'. The reward of £200 was highlighted and also the dishonourable character of the two informers. He concluded with reference to the deaths of his sister and brother and appealed to be released to 'support and console his mother in her old age'.[22]

Loyal family members continued to give support to the Craughwell prisoners and for Muldowney it came from his uncle, Michael Mahon, his brother, Patrick

---

19 NAI CSO RP 1884/6005, 3 Mar. 1884. **20** George Henry Cadogan (1840–1915) succeeded his father as 5th earl in 1873. Conservative, introduced 1887 Land Act. Resigned in 1902. **21** NAI CRF misc. 1903/484. **22** Ibid.

Muldowney, and brothers-in-law, John McDonald and Patrick Cryan. Mahon also requested Jasper Tully, MP for Roscommon,[23] to bring the case to parliament, which he did on two occasions, in 1896 and again in 1897. On the latter occasion, he asked the chief secretary, now Gerald William Balfour, whether Muldowney's case would be considered for clemency at the time of Queen Victoria's Golden Jubilee. Balfour's crushing reply was: 'I know of no reason for extending to this prisoner any exceptional treatment'. In May 1897, Michael Mahon presented another petition. He quoted from previous submissions and also linked the appeal to the queen's jubilee. Within one week, the familiar answer from the lord lieutenant was recorded in the prison file. In October 1897, Muldowney was transferred to Cork Male Prison and he remained there until June 1898 when he returned to Mountjoy. The difficulties associated with travel to Cork meant that there were no family visits during his time there.

Finnegan had made another attempt to mobilize parliamentary support for his cause in July 1897, when he requested permission to write a letter to Timothy Harrington MP, a request that was promptly refused. In January 1898, he was allowed to write to the Galway representative, David Sheehy MP, but Sheehy did not reply.

In May 1898, a petition on Muldowney's behalf was signed by his parents and his uncle Michael Mahon, Bishop Clancy of Elphin, Bishop Hoare of Ardagh, and twenty-six magistrates, poor law guardians and gentry of Cos Sligo, Leitrim and Longford. The signatures included those of James Nelson and John White, jury members at the trials, Bernard Colleary, MP for Sligo, Patrick McHugh, mayor of Sligo and the earl and countess of Granard. The points emphasized in the petition were the reward offered for information in the case and the evidence of Raftery's wife that contradicted the statements of her husband. It also stated that the attorney general and the crown counsel,

> by consenting to a plea of *nolle prosequi* in a case of this magnitude, have at length arrived at the conclusion that the evidence was unreliable and that the lives and liberties of their fellow men ought not to be imperilled on statements so obviously untrustworthy.

In the same month, a petition on behalf of both prisoners was signed by the local clergy, John Lambert of Aggard and people from Craughwell, including Patrick Cawley, Peter, Edward and Patrick Morrissey, Michael Clasby, Thomas and Michael Connolly (one of the released prisoners), John Cunniffe and Finnegan's brother Tim. The petition was summarily dismissed. Later that year, when Finnegan had been in prison for fifteen years and nine months, an almost

23 Jasper Tully, MP 1892–1906, proprietor of *Roscommon Herald*. In 1890, as editor of the paper, he was sentenced to six months imprisonment for publishing an article deemed to be intimidatory.

identical petition was rejected on the day of its submission. In November 1899, Finnegan made another attempt, citing the lapse of the Prevention of Crime (Ireland) Act of 1882, under which he was tried and that if the trial was held at the present time he would be tried by his peers and in his own county. Finnegan quoted a statement of Lord Denman[24] in the O'Connell conspiracy trial of 1844 to the effect that 'trial by special jury in Ireland was a mockery, a delusion and a snare'. He referred in detail to the practice of jury packing and the rejection of the jury panel by Chief Baron Christopher Palles in Sligo in 1886. However, the appeal fell on deaf ears and on 17 November the under secretary, Sir James B. Dougherty, recorded the verdict of Lord Cadogan: 'the law must take its course'.

Finnegan received support from his brother Tim and his niece Mary, and the visits of faithful friends such as Patrick Cawley, Michael Clasby, Michael Carr (Killora), Patrick C. Kelly, Thomas Hennelly (Athenry), Thomas Connolly (Rathcosgrove), John Newell (Caheradine) and many others must have been a great source of comfort and encouragement. His friends were able to offer him strong reassurance that the fight for his release would continue and in 1898 they formed a Prisoners Amnesty Association in Craughwell. At the same time, the Galway Social Club in Boston established a similar organization.

The activities of the PAA were monitored by the police and a report by Sergeant J. O'Connor (Ballinasloe) indicated that there were fifty members. He identified the following officers: Patrick Connolly (president); Martin Hallinan (treasurer); Patrick Rooney (secretary).[25] The report named Connolly and Hallinan as IRB members who were intimate with Finnegan before his conviction and the report claimed that a sum of £3 10s. had already been subscribed by members. John O'Loughlin (Loughrea), an IRB member, had visited Craughwell on 8 July 1900 when he attended a meeting of the PAA. The first resolution passed by the meeting solicited the aid of every public board in the county to pass resolutions for the speedy release of Finnegan and Muldowney, who were now 'over seventeen years suffering penal servitude for a crime we believe they were innocent of'. There was a particular appeal to the MPs for Co. Galway and also to John Redmond, Timothy Harrington, John Dillon and William O'Brien, who were urged to bring the case to parliament at every opportunity. John Roche MP (Woodford) was asked to bring the case before the next meeting of the Irish Parliamentary Party and to ask 'why these two innocent men should not have a revision of their life sentence'.[26]

A petition for the release of the prisoners was prepared and plans were made to mobilize the support of every public board in the county for the prisoners' release. The local press gave prominence to the agitation for the release of the

---

24 Baron Thomas Denman (1779–1854), lord chief justice (1832–50). Cited in D.S. Johnson, 'Trial by jury in Ireland 1860–1914', *Journal of Legal History*, 17:3 (Dec. 1996), 270–93. **25** NAI CBS, 22357/S, Sergeant J. O'Connor to county inspector. **26** *Galway Free Press*, 12 July 1900.

Craughwell prisoners and provided details of the circumstances surrounding their conviction. In particular, the *Western News* in an editorial referred to a deputation from the Craughwell PAA to Galway County Council asking for their support for the release of the prisoners. The county council readily agreed to petition the lord lieutenant in a memorial 'of the whole people of the Co. Galway, who are solemnly and reasonably, and rightly convinced, that the crime was not committed by the two men who have endured eighteen years penal servitude for it'.[27]

The other local authorities also responded in impressive fashion with the passage of resolutions by the Loughrea Board of Poor Law Guardians, proposed by Martin Hallinan and seconded by Thomas Connolly, urging the release of the prisoners 'who have suffered enough to satisfy the ends of justice'. The only dissenting voice was that of a Mr Villiers. The Portumna Board of Poor Law Guardians and the Loughrea Town Commissioners, the rural district councils of Galway, Gort, Portumna, Ballinasloe, Mountbellew and Oughterard, and the urban councils of Galway and Ballinasloe passed similar resolutions. The resolution of the Ballinasloe Urban Council was noteworthy because of the support of Dr Rutherford, an ardent Unionist. The response to this flurry of activity came from Under Secretary Sir James B. Dougherty on 8 September 1900: 'the lords justices in a full consideration of all the circumstances of the case, their excellencies have decided that the law must take its course'.

The monitoring of the local press by the vigilant Sergeant J. O'Connor discovered a letter in the *Tuam News* that made an impassioned plea for mercy for the Craughwell prisoners from William J. (Willy) Duffy, Loughrea.[28] In the course of the letter, Duffy reviewed the doubtful nature of the guilty verdicts and the tainted evidence that procured them. He castigated David Sheehy MP for his failure to respond to a letter from Finnegan and also Timothy Harrington MP for his failure to take an interest in the case. Duffy concluded by stating that 'the lot of these two men calls for energetic action. Galway County, from end to end, should stir itself, and by resolution at its public boards and public meetings, call the attention of the world to the cruel, inhuman treatment of these poor men'. In the report to Dublin Castle that accompanied the press cutting, Sergeant O'Connor claimed that Duffy was an active nationalist and county secretary of the Gaelic Athletic Association and he alleged that he was a member of the Loughrea IRB Circle and 'an aspirant for the county leadership of the IRB'.[29]

During 1900, Finnegan exchanged three letters with his friend Michael Clasby and may have been informed of the remarkable statement made by John Doherty about the killing of his cousin Peter in 1881, in which he affirmed Finnegan's innocence (see above, p. 82).

27 *Western News*, 21 July 1900; *Tuam News*, 21 July 1900; *Galway Free Press*, 21 July 1900.
28 *Tuam News*, 23 June 1900. 29 NAI CBS (1900) 158S in CRF misc. 1903/484.

THE GENERAL ELECTION CONVENTION FOR SOUTH GALWAY, 1900

During the late nineteenth century, the practice of nominating prisoners to contest seats in parliament was adopted in order to focus attention on the plight of imprisoned nationalists. The tactic was first employed in 1869, when O'Donovan Rossa was selected for the election in Tipperary. John Mitchel was elected for the same constituency in 1875 but the election was declared void. While Michael Davitt was in Portland Prison, he was elected MP for Meath in 1882 and subsequently disqualified. John Daly was similarly excluded in 1895. The practice was again employed at the convention for the general election of 1900 that was convened to select a candidate for south Galway. It was held in the Loughrea courthouse on 3 October. Every parish in the constituency was represented and it proved to be an occasion of high drama. Peter J. Kelly (Killeenadeema) was elected chairman and commenced by paying tribute to Peter Sweeney,[30] who had chaired the preparatory meeting on 25 August, but who had died following a road accident during September. Apologies for inability to attend were recorded from some local clergy including Revd J. O'Donovan CC.[31] The chairman informed the meeting of a parliamentary pledge forwarded from the United Irish League[32] Directory, binding the selected candidate to act and vote with the majority of the Irish Parliamentary Party.[33] When the name of David Sheehy was mentioned, there were several interruptions from the audience relating to his failure to help the Craughwell prisoners. Yet, Sheehy, who was the sitting MP, was the first candidate nominated. The proposer was the chairman, Peter Kelly, and the seconder was Michael F. Hogan, chairman of the Loughrea Board of Poor Law Guardians. Hogan referred to Sheehy's distinguished record in nationalist politics in the past, but also mentioned Sheehy's neglect of Galway during the past ten years. The second nomination was that of Willy Duffy, Loughrea, who was proposed by Martin Ward[34] and seconded by Denis Cunningham. Michael Clasby (Craughwell) then claimed the floor and urged that the candidate selected should pledge himself 'to work energetically inside and outside parliament for the speedy liberation of the Craughwell prisoners, Michael Muldowney and Patrick Finnegan'.[35] This remark was greeted by loud and prolonged cheering. Thomas Corbett, chairman

---

30 Peter Sweeney, Loughrea, brother of John Sweeney, was imprisoned as a suspect in 1882. Elected a member of the first Galway county council in 1898.   31 Leading proponent of the Celtic Revival and influential in selecting artwork for St Brendan's Cathedral, Loughrea. Later became famous as the author Gerald O'Donovan.   32 The United Irish League was founded in Westport in Jan. 1898 by William O'Brien, MP for Mallow and Cork city, 1893–1918. He was a veteran of the Land War and the Plan of Campaign in the 1880s. The UIL was committed to the redistribution of grazing land. *United Irish League: constitution and rules*, quoted in Fergus Campbell, *Land and revolution* (Oxford, 2005), pp 127–30.   33 *Western News*, 6 Oct. 1900.   34 Ward played a leading part in local nationalist politics and was at the centre of a major controversy when he was evicted by Lord Clanrickarde in 1905.   35 *Western News*, 6 Oct. 1900.

of the Craughwell PAA and a member of Galway County Council, proposed Patrick Finnegan. During his speech, he cited precedents for selecting a prisoner as an election candidate. In seconding the proposal, Clasby gave a description of the trial and the characters of the informers. In accepting the nomination, the chairman said that in 1886 Parnell had asked him if he could guarantee that the prisoners were innocent and he had replied that he could.[36] At that stage, he withdrew Sheehy's name in favour of Finnegan. Duffy addressed the meeting and, in concluding, said that he was withdrawing his name in favour of Finnegan. John Roche MP, Woodford, said that he 'yielded to no man his anxiety that justice be done to the prisoners, Finnegan and Muldowney'. But 'unfortunately Finnegan was not qualified and he would say unhesitatingly that if he were he would be the first man to support him'. In the event of his success in the election, Roche feared that there was nothing to prevent a man like Edward Shaw Tener[37] or anybody like him to annul the nomination. Revd Egan, PP of Duniry, suggested that another nationalist be nominated with Finnegan to contest the election. He thought that 'if they wished to make a protest against jury packing, which was the greatest curse of English rule, they should elect the man that was convicted by a packed jury in Sligo'. The chairman put Finnegan's name to the meeting and he was unanimously selected. John Roche MP said that the question now was which of the other candidates would be put forward 'in case it was attempted by the enemy to get the constituency'. The result was that Duffy received 110 votes and Sheehy received thirty-seven.

The election was uncontested and, as Finnegan was not qualified to take the seat, Duffy was elected unopposed. The main purpose of the selection of Finnegan as a candidate was to generate publicity for the cause of liberating the Craughwell prisoners and this was certainly achieved. At the meeting of the south Galway executive of the UIL on 13 November, Michael Clasby proposed and Patrick Cawley seconded a resolution requesting Duffy to bring the case of the Craughwell prisoners before the Irish Parliamentary Party convention on 11 December. In reply, Duffy stated that 'any efforts within his power would be used in securing the relief of these two innocent men, who were now close on twenty years in prison'. Duffy's pledge would prove to be an important element in the promotion of their cause inside and outside parliament and his first action was to propose a resolution of support for the prisoners at the Irish Parliamentary Party convention in Dublin. The proposal was passed with acclamation with the agreement to bring it before parliament early in 1901.

36 There is no record that Parnell intervened in the case at that time and the Craughwell prisoners were not mentioned in the parliamentary debates on miscarriages of justice in 1885. 37 Agent for Lord Clanrickarde.

AGITATION FOR RELEASE OF THE CRAUGHWELL PRISONERS, 1900–3

Following his visit to Mountjoy on 8 October 1900, Michael Clasby had attempted to see Timothy Harrington MP, but he was away on business. Instead, Clasby had a long interview with Michael Davitt. Davitt told Clasby that he highly approved of all the Craughwell PAA had done, including the returning of Finnegan as MP for south Galway to let the world see the high respect in which he was held by the people who always and now fully believed in his innocence. A copy of a letter written by Clasby, dated 23 December 1900,[38] reassured Finnegan that 'he would never be forgotten by his friends', despite the rejection of the petitions from the local authorities. Davitt promised that he would do all he could to help his case. Clasby also referred to the kindness of the prison governor in allowing Finnegan to write more letters than his strict entitlement. Meanwhile, in March 1900, Muldowney was transferred to Maryborough prison to serve the remainder of his sentence and, in October that year, another appeal by him for release was rejected.

After his election, Willy Duffy lost little time in bringing the case before the House of Commons. In March 1901, he tabled a question for the new chief secretary, George Wyndham, who had succeeded Gerald Balfour in November 1900. Details of the Craughwell prisoners' case were presented, as well as reference to the petitions from the representative public bodies. In his reply,[39] Wyndham merely stated that the lord lieutenant had decided, as recently as August 1900, that the law must take its course. He then had recourse to the traditional ploy of stating that if any new fact had transpired since then it could be brought before the lord lieutenant. John Redmond intervened to suggest that Wyndham might use his influence with the lord lieutenant, but Wyndham replied: 'I am afraid I could not. It would be altogether outside my sphere'. Duffy also availed of a brief opportunity to raise the release of the prisoners on the eve of the recess of parliament, but the speaker who moved the closure of the session terminated his speech.[40] A debate on jury packing was the occasion of Duffy's maiden speech and he made full use of the opportunity. A press report described the speech as 'the ablest maiden speech from the Irish benches; it was cogent and eloquent beyond measure'.[41] Duffy was prevented from naming the prisoners, but he put on record his own fate in Wicklow in 1888 at the hands of a Protestant jury that was constituted on exactly the same lines as the Sligo juries. He outlined the history of the Craughwell case and asked 'was the

38 Letter in possession of Gerry Cloonan, Caherfurvaus, Craughwell.   **39** Documentation prepared in Dublin Castle and sent to the Irish office in relation to the parliamentary question referred to the absence of the official reports dealing with events subsequent to the murder of Peter Doherty and prior to the arrest of Finnegan and Muldowney. This was the file, NAI CSO RP1884/6005, issued to DI Alan Bell in Mar. 1884 (see above, pp 110–11).   **40** *Galway Observer*, 6 Apr. 1901.   **41** *Galway Observer*, 11 May 1901.

vengeance of the government not yet satisfied?' He referred to the 'cold, calculated, callous and stereotyped reply to his parliamentary question' and said 'what
rank humbug and hypocrisy it was for the attorney general for Ireland[42] to stand
up and taunt the nationalists with being disloyal to the constitution which
practised and inflicted such disgraceful infamies on their people'.[43]

Very little of the prison correspondence has survived apart from two letters
from Finnegan in 1901. Writing to Michael Clasby on 10 April, he said that the
efforts to secure his release left him in the best of spirits and he expressed grati-
tude regarding Willy Duffy's efforts on his behalf and pride in 'our valiant
representative in parliament'. Finnegan was transferred from Mountjoy Jail to
Maryborough Jail on 20 April 1901, and during that summer, writing to his niece
Mary, he said that he was able to take an interest in work on the farm and
commented that 'the potatoes were as big as turnips with no sign of blight'.

The case of the Craughwell prisoners was regularly mentioned at meetings of
the executive of the south Galway UIL, and during the summer of 1901 there
were further petitions from local authorities, including a resolution from Galway
County Council that had been proposed by James W. Ffrench and seconded by
Thomas Corbett.

Willy Duffy's next project was the generation of a memorial signed by
members of the House of Commons, including sixty-five members of the Irish
Parliamentary Party and six MPs from Britain including Keir Hardie, the
founder of the British Labour Party.[44] The memorial was sent to Dublin Castle
on 25 July 1901 and was acknowledged by Lord Plunkett, the assistant under
secretary. In a reply to Willy Duffy, dated 30 August, Plunkett referred to the
'influentially signed memorial and stated that the lord lieutenant had considered
the cases from time to time when he was in Ireland'. Later on, in a cryptic
comment, Plunkett stated that

> His Excellency[45] feels sure that you will recognize that the subject of the
> exercise of the Royal Prerogative of Mercy is not one upon which it
> would be proper for him to enter into a correspondence; and he regrets
> that he is unable to make a premature announcement with reference to
> the decision at which he arrived some time ago.[46]

Willy Duffy kept the issue alive and a detailed article in the *Independent and
Nation* on 18 June was duly noted by Dublin Castle. An accompanying editorial
urged the remission of the sentences in commemoration of the forthcoming
coronation of King Edward.

---

42 John Atkinson QC, MP. 43 *Galway Observer*, 18 May 1901. 44 NAI CRF misc.
1903/396. 45 Lord Cadogan. 46 *Western News*, 18 Jan. 1902.

RELEASE OF PATRICK FINNEGAN

At last, on 9 July 1902, the order for Finnegan's release was initialled by Lord Cadogan and signed by George Wyndham and two days later he was released on licence. A formal note was sent from Dublin Castle to John Redmond MP, leader of the Irish Parliamentary Party, to acquaint him and the other petitioners that Patrick Finnegan was to be released on 11 July, a full year after their petition was submitted.

The conditions for release specified in the licence were that:

- the holder shall preserve his licence and produce it when called upon to do so by a magistrate or police officer;
- he shall abstain from any violation of the law;
- he shall not habitually associate with notoriously bad characters, such as reputed thieves and prostitutes;
- he shall not lead an idle and dissolute life, without visible means of obtaining an honest livelihood;
- if his licence is forfeited or revoked in consequence of a conviction for any offence, he will be liable to undergo a term of penal servitude equal to the remaining portion of his life.

Finnegan informed Michael Clasby of his release by letter and notified him that he would arrive in Athenry station on the 1.15pm train from Broadstone on 12 July. On arrival, he was greeted by a crowd of friends and taken to Murphy's Hotel for refreshments. He was driven to Craughwell and given a great reception there with bonfires, illuminations and brass bands. A meeting was held and Michael Clasby, his faithful friend throughout his prison ordeal, read the formal address of welcome on behalf of the nationalists of south Galway. Willy Duffy MP, who had made such strenuous efforts to secure his release, joined in the celebrations.[47]

CAMPAIGN FOR MULDOWNEY'S RELEASE

Muldowney had petitioned for release in October 1901 and February 1902 without success. Another appeal was rejected in June 1902 and the news of Finnegan's release, without any indication of mercy for himself, must have been a bitter blow. The two prisoners met just before Finnegan's departure, their only meeting during the lengthy imprisonment. The press reported that their parting was a most affectionate and cordial one.[48]

47 *Freeman's Journal*, 15 July 1902, *Galway Observer*, 19 July 1902; *Western News*, 26 July 1902.
48 *Galway Observer*, 19 July 1902.

Finnegan's release led to renewed efforts on Muldowney's behalf. In July and August 1902, Leitrim County Council and the district councils of Mohill and Castlerea passed resolutions for his release. Jasper Tully raised the Craughwell case in the House of Commons on 28 July and, in reply, George Wyndham, the chief secretary, stated that Muldowney's release would take place as soon as a new lord lieutenant was installed. Lord Dudley was appointed to succeed Lord Cadogan on 11 August and he was installed on 16 August. But there was no evidence of an early intervention in the case. On the same occasion, Tully also asked the chief secretary if a constable named Redington appeared as a witness in the prosecution of Muldowney and Finnegan and if he would state his present rank and where he was stationed. Wyndham replied that Redington was a witness in the Craughwell case and that he was promoted to the rank of DI in 1897. He was now stationed in Granard, Co. Longford.[49] Tully had addressed a meeting of the UIL held in Bornacoola, Co. Leitrim, in October 1901,[50] and on that occasion he referred to the Craughwell case and the fact that John McDonald, a brother-in-law of Michael Muldowney, was on the platform. He also commented on a recent case in which perjured evidence given by a Sergeant Sheridan had resulted in the conviction of an innocent man for an outrage in Ballinamore. Sergeant Sheridan had subsequently left the country and Tully identified Redington as the DI in charge of the case, the implication being that, if Redington was capable of fabricating false evidence in the Craughwell case, he could also have condoned it in the Ballinamore case.

On 6 August 1902 in the House of Commons, Willy Duffy and Jasper Tully called attention to the continuing imprisonment of Muldowney. They appealed for his release and suggested that 'to detain him there longer would be a cruel act of vengeance unworthy of any humane administration'. It is extraordinary that, rather than adopt a humane approach to the question, Wyndham decided instead to attack the petitioners. He said that

> anyone listening to the appeals for mercy for Muldowney could not but come to the conclusion that he had been most unfortunate in his advocates. An appeal for mercy could not be based upon desperate accusations being made against other men, as was done by honourable members opposite. He might say, however, as regards the exercise of the prerogative of mercy, that as far as he could see, there was no such great discrepancy between the facts of Muldowney's case and that of Finnegan's as would warrant the expectation that Muldowney's imprisonment would be prolonged much beyond what it had been in the case of Finnegan.[51]

49 *Leitrim Advertiser*, 31 July 1902. 50 *Leitrim Advertiser*, 24 Oct. 1901. 51 *Freeman's Journal*, 7 Aug. 1902.

Muldowney had already petitioned twice during 1902 and his uncle, Michael Mahon, and his brother-in-law, John McDonald, sent a third petition in October. Jasper Tully referred to Wyndham's statement when he submitted the petition and he also asked Wyndham if he would state when Muldowney would be released. Wyndham replied that he had brought the case to the notice of the lord lieutenant and 'had no reason to believe that there would be any considerable difference in the total period of imprisonment undergone by the two men referred to'.[52]

Willy Duffy continued to take an interest in the case, and on 13 November he visited Muldowney in Maryborough Jail. Tully tabled a further parliamentary question on 18 November, and on this occasion the reply indicated that the case 'will be specially considered by him [the lord lieutenant] on 23 January 1903'. In fact, Lord Dudley had already written to Lord Ashbourne, the lord chancellor, on 15 November, informing him that 'unless he had any objection, he proposed to release Muldowney on licence on that date which would be twenty years from the date of his original arrest – tho' his sentence does not properly count 'till 11 July 1884'.[53] This was the date of his conviction. Wyndham signed the order for Muldowney's release on licence on 19 January 1903. He left Maryborough on 23 January 1903 and travelled to Co. Leitrim to join his relatives in Johnston's Bridge, Dromod.

The duration of the Craughwell prisoners' confinement in prison was approximately the same. From the date of his arrest in 1883, Muldowney had served 19 years, 11 months and 13 days compared with Finnegan's 19 years, 5 months and 13 days. If one takes into account his two other periods in jail before sentence, Finnegan's total confinement was 19 years, 10 months and 24 days.

Various opinions were voiced during the nineteenth century regarding the duration of a sentence of life imprisonment. In 1865, Attorney General James Lawson believed that in a case of deliberate murder, the convict 'should not under any circumstances be set at liberty'.[54] Three years later, Attorney General Robert Warren expressed the opinion that a commuted sentence 'may properly be brought under the consideration of the govt after an interval of 10 or 12 years from conviction'.[55] However, in 1882, in response to a petition for release of a convict, the atorney general, William Johnson, 'alluded to a new rule: usually observed is that the cases of convicts whose death sentences have been commuted to penal servitude for life, are not considered for licence until they have served 20 years'.[56] It would appear, therefore, that the duration of the prisoners' sentences was predetermined and that the petitions and parliamentary questions and debates had no effect on the implacable judgment: 'the law must take its course'.

52 *Freeman's Journal*, 29 Oct. 1902. **53** NAI CRF misc. 1903/484. **54** NAI CRF/1885/McLoughlin/18 in Vaughan (2009), p. 326. **55** Ibid. **56** Ibid.

9 The years of freedom

MICHAEL MULDOWNEY

On the day following his release, Muldowney submitted a request to be released unconditionally rather than on licence. He referred to the long duration of the sentence and that an additional penalty imposed by the conditions of the licence was not justified. He also commented on the appeal on his behalf by RIC colleagues at the time of his conviction in 1884. The lord chancellor rejected the appeal. An annotation in the file, written by the under secretary, Sir James B. Dougherty, claimed that the county inspector of the RIC was convinced at the time that 'the police had no part in getting up or forwarding' the petition. The callous treatment of Muldowney persisted therefore to the very end of his prison ordeal.

In March 1903, Lord Granard wrote to Lord Plunkett and referred to the large number of people, including his father, who were confident of Muldowney's innocence at the time of the trial, and of his exemplary conduct in prison. Lord Granard stated that he thought he had found a very good opening for Muldowney in Australia and he requested 'rescindment of the obligation to report to the police following his release'.[1] The opinion of the General Prisons Board was sought, and they replied:

> If the police authorities see no objection, the board think this is a case in which the obligation of reporting to the police may be remitted. The proposal to send the convict to Australia is not one which should be endorsed or countenanced in any way officially. It is quite certain that if the police in the Australia colonies know that he is a convict, he will not be permitted to land.

The final record in the prison file of Michael Muldowney was a report from DI R.A. Madden (Mohill), who notified Dublin Castle of the emigration of Michael Muldowney to America on 7 September 1903. Muldowney lived in New Jersey and worked as a carpenter, a trade he learned in prison. He married a woman from Sligo, but they had no children. He enjoyed a very happy life in America; he forgave his jailers and did not dwell on the miscarriage of justice that had blighted his life for twenty years. At a family baptism in America in the 1930s, he held the infant and said 'I am as innocent as that new-born child and I am very pleased indeed to see him', echoing a statement he made in Sligo after his conviction a half a century earlier.

1 NAI CRF misc. 1903/484.

PATRICK FINNEGAN

Patrick Finnegan's political involvement at home
On his return home, Patrick Finnegan would be forgiven for thinking that little
had changed in Craughwell during his long period of imprisonment. At the time
of his arrest in December 1882, the Irish National League had commenced the
second phase of the Land War and, on his release in 1902, the recently formed
United Irish League had mounted a formidable campaign against graziers. The
UIL was founded in 1898 by William O'Brien and its *Constitution*, published in
1900, had three objectives: the abolition of landlordism by means of a compulsory system of sale, the reinstatement of evicted tenants and the abolition of the
grazing system.[2] The tactical features of the previous land agitation also
emerged, with boycotting and intimidation of those taking over an evicted farm,
graziers and land grabbers. The police districts of Loughrea and Athenry were
at the centre of the agitation and Craughwell was once again in the forefront. In
a speech to the south Galway executive of the UIL on 9 September 1901, Willy
Duffy quoted comments of George Wyndham in the House of Commons, in
which he singled out Craughwell for special attention:

> There was one spot alone in all Ireland which gave him any cause for
> uneasiness, that there was one division where the people were really
> determined on putting down grazing and its concomitant evils and that
> there was one place which he was determined to grapple with.[3]

During the campaign, a number of members of the Craughwell UIL branch
were arrested and charged with unlawful conspiracy to prevent the taking or
occupying of grazing lands. The Craughwell prisoners on this occasion included
Michael Clasby, Patrick Cawley, John Newell and John Connolly (of Cahercrin).
All of them had been prominently associated with the Land War in the 1880s.
The law officers of the crown decided that, in view of the intimidation of
witnesses, there was no reasonable prospect of success and they abandoned the
prosecution.[4]

Within a few weeks of his release from prison, Finnegan attended a meeting
of the Craughwell branch of the UIL and was unanimously elected chairman.[5]
The local police noted this development and it was immediately reported to
Dublin Castle, a reminder to Finnegan of his status as a prisoner released on
licence.

A meeting of the nationalists of Galway was held in Loughrea in August
under the chairmanship of Willy Duffy. The purpose of the meeting was to set

---

2 *United Irish League: constitution and rules*, quoted in Campbell, *Land and revolution*, p. 127.
3 *Western News*, 14 Sept. 1901. 4 Campbell, *Land and revolution*, pp 67–9. 5 *Tuam Herald*, 9
Aug. 1902.

11 Patrick Finnegan, from Patrick J. Finnegan, *An Irish patriot, victim of the English government* (New York, 1904). Archival reprint by Ventura Pacific Ltd, California.

up a fund for the support of Finnegan, who was now penniless. Duffy became chairman of the fund, Michael Clasby was secretary and John Farrell acted as treasurer. Successful collections were reported throughout south Galway and sums of money were also received from Boston and New York. At a function in Craughwell in July 1903,[6] Finnegan was presented with a cheque for £300 and shortly afterwards he emigrated to America.

Patrick Finnegan in America 1903–5
Soon after his arrival in Boston, Finnegan was the guest of honour at a reception organized by the Galway Social Club and held in Wells Memorial Hall. The report in the *Boston Pilot* referred to a large attendance of representatives of the various Irish–American organizations.[7] The president of the Galway Social Club introduced Mr P.A. Murray of Newton, the presiding officer, who claimed to

6 *Irish World and American Industrial Liberator*, 4 July 1903.   7 *Boston Pilot*, 25 July 1903.

have known Finnegan as a boy in Ireland. In his speech, Finnegan gave details of the trials and his introduction to the hangman, James Berry, on the train journey to Galway. He recounted the indignities visited upon him in prison because he was 'a land league prisoner'. Patrick Sarsfield Cunniffe read an address on behalf of the social club that expressed admiration for Finnegan's heroism and wished him a long life and happiness in America.

The political speeches that night reflected the tensions between Clan na Gael and the constitutional organizations. M.J. Coyle, president of the Parnell Club, was introduced as a representative of Clan na Gael and he stated his belief that constitutional agitation would never win Irish freedom. On the other hand, John O'Callaghan, national secretary of the UIL of America, linked the aims of that organization with the antecedent land league organizations of the 1880s and reminded the meeting that it was as land leaguers that Patrick Finnegan, Francis Hynes, Patrick Walsh, Sylvester Poff and James Barrett in Kerry and John Twiss in Cork were sentenced to death. At the end of the formal proceedings, Finnegan was presented with a gold Waltham watch.

Shortly afterwards, on 23 August, Finnegan was present when Michael Clasby, who was on a holiday in America, was honoured for his efforts on behalf of the Craughwell prisoners.[8] Among the audience that night was Thomas Joyce, one of the men arrested with Finnegan and released in 1885 when the trials were abandoned. In September, Finnegan travelled to New York for a joint meeting of the Boston and New York Galway Mens Associations held in his honour in the Vanderbilt Hotel. Thomas Joyce and Michael Clasby were also present that evening.[9] During his time in Boston, Finnegan lived in Dorchester and was a member of the Dorchester branch of the Ancient Order of Hibernians.[10]

In May 1904, an article in the *Gaelic American* announced the publication of a pamphlet priced at twenty-five cents.[11] It seems probable that an Irish-American journalist wrote the pamphlet, although Finnegan was named as the author. The tone is highly polemical and the language fervently patriotic throughout and, in addition, it gives an account of Finnegan's trials and sojourn in prison that is often inaccurate. The booklet constructs an elaborate indictment of Sergeant Redington, alleging that he fabricated the story and persuaded Raftery and Moran to play their part in the plot with the promise of 'glittering gold'. It claimed that Redington tutored the informers in the memorization and recital of the fictitious account. An interesting encounter is recorded between

8 *Boston Pilot*, 9 Aug. 1903. 9 *Irish World and American Industrial Liberator*, 26 Sept. 1903.
10 The Ancient Order of Hibernians was founded in America to represent Irish nationalist interests. In Ireland, led by Joseph Devlin MP, it promoted Catholic and nationalist concerns in direct opposition to the Orange Order. 11 Patrick J. Finnegan, *The case of Patrick J. Finnegan: an Irish patriot, victim of the English government* (New York, 1904). Archival reprint by Ventura Pacific Ltd, California.

Edward Barrett, a reporter with the *Western News*, and Jack Moran in March 1883. Barrett knew that Moran was staying in the police barracks in Eglinton Street in Galway while the initial magisterial enquiries were conducted in the nearby courthouse and county jail. Barrett met Moran at the barracks' gate and said 'what are you doing here, Jack?' He then tried to persuade Moran not to give evidence against 'innocent men that he had known since boyhood'. At that point, two policemen seized Moran and dragged him back inside. The *Gaelic American* was the mouthpiece for John Devoy and Clan na Gael and it carried advertisements for the pamphlet every week until September 1905. There is no evidence to support the contention, but it is possible that the pamphlet was published by Devoy, who would have regarded the story as a propaganda coup, given its tale of British injustice inflicted on innocent Irishmen. Finnegan certainly knew Devoy in America and also Tom Clarke, who was the business manager of the *Gaelic American* at that time.

Another social function in honour of Finnegan was held in San Francisco in January 1905. On that occasion, he was presented with $500, the proceeds of a fund-raising campaign in the city.[12] In September 1905, he visited Chicago[13] to be honoured by the Henry Grattan Club. During his stay, he was the guest of Thomas Morrissey, an old friend from Craughwell.

In July 1905, Finnegan paid a visit to Butte, Montana; the destination for many Irish emigrants since the Great Famine. They included Thomas Francis Meagher, who became governor of the state. The attraction was the prospect of steady, well-paid employment in the copper mining industry. By 1900, 12,000 first- and second-generation Irish lived in the town of Butte and Silver Bow County. They formed a closely knit community based on shared nationality and religion and they played a prominent part in the political life of the city and county.[14] Two powerful political organizations represented the Irish: the Ancient Order of Hibernians, founded in 1880; and the Robert Emmet Literary Association, founded in the following year. Through their activities, the Democratic Party ruled the town and the Irish dominated the city council and public appointments.

The Robert Emmet Literary Association was the Clan na Gael camp in Butte. Clan na Gael was the American branch of the Fenians led by John Devoy and had revolutionary aims. It conducted its affairs in a secretive manner and when Finnegan attended the meetings of the association on 13 and 20 July 1905, the chairman was the senior guardian, Brother 117.[15] It is of great interest that Finnegan was introduced as a member of Camp 237, Boston, because this is the

12 *The Leader*, 7 Jan. 1905.   13 *Gaelic American*, 16 Sept. 1905.   14 For an extended account of the Irish immigrants, see David M. Emmons, *The Butte Irish* (Urbana & Chicago, 1990). 15 Butte-Silver Bow Public Archives, Robert Emmet Literary Association minute book, 13 & 20 July 1905.

only documented evidence that he was a Fenian. He spoke at length about his experiences during his long imprisonment.

Finnegan also attended three meetings of the Ancient Order of Hibernians,[16] at which many of the leading figures of political and commercial life were present. He again spoke about conditions in Ireland and his prison ordeal. Both organizations contributed $400 for his benefit.

Patrick Finnegan's return to Ireland and life in Loughrea
Finnegan returned to Craughwell at the end of 1905 and a few weeks later the *Western News* interviewed him in Loughrea.[17] It had been reported prior to Finnegan's departure from Boston that Willy Duffy was going to resign his seat in the House of Commons and that he did not intend to contest the general election of 1906. A public meeting organized by the Boston Ancient Order of Hibernians endorsed Finnegan's candidacy and their recommendation was transmitted by cable to Michael Clasby. The *Western News*, now owned and edited by William Hastings, regularly displayed considerable antipathy to Duffy and indeed to many other local public representatives. Hastings taunted Duffy with the circumstances of the 1900 convention, at which Finnegan had been nominated unanimously and then withdrew because his status as a prisoner would disqualify him. The paper also alleged that Duffy had agreed to withdraw from parliament in favour of Finnegan. At the convention held in Loughrea on 11 January 1906, all branches of the UIL were represented. It is likely that Finnegan had held discussions with Duffy beforehand and had decided not to challenge him. In fact, he proposed the motion nominating Duffy, who was then selected unopposed.[18]

In April 1906, Finnegan married Alice Sweeney and left Craughwell to live in the Sweeney home in Dunkellin Street, Loughrea. Alice was the daughter of John Sweeney, one of the leading stalwarts of both phases of the Land War, who had died in 1899. After his death, his widow Bridget (née O'Neill) operated their public house and grocery shop. Sweeney and Finnegan had been prisoners together in Galway Jail as suspects under the 1881 Protection of Person and Property (Ireland) Act from April to August 1882. Sweeney was an active supporter of the campaign to gather funds for the Craughwell Prisoners' Defence Fund in 1883–4 and he was the recipient of the statement of John Doherty that declared his belief that Finnegan was innocent of the killing of Peter Doherty.

The first child of Patrick Finnegan and Alice Sweeney was a daughter, Hanna, born in August 1907, followed by Patrick John (P.J.) in 1908. Another son, Thomas, was born in 1912 and died soon afterwards. Alice suffered from

---

16 Butte-Silver Bow Public Archives, Ancient Order of Hibernians minute book, 10, 12, 17 & 19 July 1905. 17 *Western News*, 6 Jan. 1906. 18 *Western News*, 13 Jan. 1906.

tuberculosis and family letters expressed concerns about her health on many occasions during her marriage. Her condition deteriorated and she died at the age of thirty-five on 1 May 1912. She was buried in Garrybreeda cemetery. The licence for the public house was in the name of Alice Sweeney and, as his status was that of a convicted person, Finnegan was debarred from holding the licence. He therefore sent a petition to the lord lieutenant requesting a pardon. The petition was supported by a letter from Willy Duffy to Sir James B. Dougherty, the under secretary, that referred to Finnegan's irreproachable character and the burden now placed upon him of raising his young family. DI Leonard (Loughrea) was asked for a report and he stated that he had known Finnegan for five years and that he lived an honest life. He also referred to Finnegan's political activities and association with well known members of the UIL. The opinion of the attorney general was sought and he stated 'that the sentence is a just one and it would not appear to me to be right to grant a pardon for an indirect purpose such as this'. Again, 'the law must take its course'. The original injustice was to persist and Finnegan never again petitioned for its redress.[19]

Earning a living became an important consideration, and in November 1906 the Loughrea District Council proposed him for the position of county rate collector for the Loughrea area. A member of the council, Martin Griffin[20] (Gurteen), on behalf of his son, carried out an extensive canvas for the votes of county councillors. Finnegan decided to withdraw his nomination on the understanding that he would be given the next vacant position.[21] He sought the position of returning officer for the local government election of 1908 and was proposed by P.J. Kelly (Killeenadeema), and seconded by Pat Larkin (Kiltormer). He was selected unanimously when two other candidates withdrew in his favour. The elections were held in June 1908 and Finnegan submitted a bill for £1,576 that was reduced to £1,450 with his agreement. When all expenses were paid, he was able to lodge the substantial sum of £1,007 to his bank account. Whenever he sought appointments of this nature, his supporters laid considerable emphasis on the privations endured by him because of his unjust conviction and imprisonment.

Finnegan became active in the UIL and in March 1906 he was a member of the Political Prisoners Indemnity Fund that was set up jointly by the UIL and the GAA.[22] The immediate case of relevance was the defence of those arrested in connection with the shooting at Mr Shawe-Taylor and his wife at Lisnagranchy near Ardrahan. In April 1907 he was a member of the Loughrea Town Tenants Association, whose main activities involved arbitration in disputes over rent and in later years the purchase of the leasehold of Loughrea town, a part of the Clanrickarde estate. Although the branch of the TTA in

19 NAI CSO RP 1912/16042. 20 A member of the Griffin family who were actively involved in the Land War. His son, Fr Griffin, was assassinated during the War of Independence. 21 *Western News*, 3 Nov. 1906. 22 *Western News*, 17 Mar. 1906.

Athenry became closely associated with the Sinn Féin organization,[23] press accounts of the Loughrea branch's activities provide no support for a similar connection.

Finnegan became vice president of the Loughrea branch of the UIL in 1909 and he represented the branch on the executive committee for south Galway. At that time, the UIL was still actively involved in the 'Ranch War' that had been described a few years earlier by the county inspector of the RIC as 'a most pernicious body, being the origin of intimidation and outrage throughout the surrounding country'.[24] At a meeting of the executive in September 1909, Finnegan said that he had in his possession the balance of the defence fund set up in 1906 and it had been suggested that he should hand it over to the current Craughwell Prisoners Defence Committee for the defence of Michael Dermody and Thomas Hynes, who were arrested in connection with the shooting of Constable Goldrick at Craughwell in January 1909.[25] It is ironic that Finnegan had money for this purpose, having benefited from a similarly named fund a quarter of a century earlier. In addition, it was widely believed that Dermody and Hynes were innocent of the crime and in fact neither was convicted.

In January 1910, Finnegan was successful in the election for Loughrea Town Commissioners, on which body he served for three years. He was also a candidate for the position of returning officer for that year's county council elections, and the nomination was strongly supported by Willy Duffy MP, the UIL executive and the Loughrea district council.[26] The appointment gave rise to lively exchanges at the quarterly meeting of the county council and, following a vote, he was defeated by William O'Malley (Kilmilkin), a brother of a serving councillor.

In 1906, the UIL in Craughwell had split into two factions that became known as the 'Hallinanites' and the 'Kennyites', named after their leaders, Martin Hallinan and Tom Kenny. A nationalist meeting was held in Craughwell on 26 November 1910 and, in his speech, Willy Duffy MP strongly appealed to the people 'to sink all their differences for the common good'. Hallinan assured the meeting that Craughwell stood at the back of the UIL and the Irish Parliamentary Party and he referred to the benefits that had already occurred in the area, with the sale of the Lambert, Graham and St Clerans estates. It is significant that Kenny was not allowed to speak at the meeting, but a letter was read out that expressed his dissatisfaction and his decision to withdraw from the branch's activities.[27] An attempt to achieve reconciliation between the two factions was made by the officers of the UIL executive and reported to the AGM in January 1912. Willy Duffy said he had visited Craughwell, accompanied by Finnegan, Martin Ward and Joe Gilchrist, and in the course of their meeting

23 Campbell, *Land and revolution*, pp 115–16.   24 Campbell, *Land and revolution*, p. 135.
25 *Connaught Tribune*, 18 Sept. 1909.   26 *Connaught Tribune*, 22 Oct. 1910.   27 *Connaught Tribune*, 3 Dec. 1910.

with representatives of the two factions, a resolution was passed in favour of the need for reconciliation. However, Kenny had refused to rejoin the organization. The split was never healed, with the Hallinan faction remaining dominant until 1918 and Kenny becoming involved with Sinn Féin.[28]

Regular meetings of the Loughrea TTA were held, and by March 1910 Finnegan had become chairman of the branch. In his address to the August meeting in 1911, he referred to their success in settling disputes and the need for a court of arbitration that would fix fair rents on houses similar to the arrangements for tenant farmers.[29] In 1915, their attention turned to the Clanrickarde estate. Lord Clanrickarde had resisted all attempts at compulsory purchase and still owned the towns of Loughrea and Portumna. Following a decision of the land court in 1915, the estate was handed over to the Congested Districts Board and Clanrickarde was paid the sum of £238,211. Loughrea TTA passed a resolution that Loughrea town be included in the sale, as well as the grazing lands adjacent to the town, for distribution among the townspeople. The CDB replied that Loughrea and Portumna were not included in the sale of the estate[30] and, in a further communication, Sir Henry Doran of the CDB informed the TTA that the holdings could be sold if Lord Clanrickarde wished.[31]

His narrow defeat in the election for Loughrea Town Commissioners in January 1913 meant that Finnegan could apply for the position of town steward. He was appointed in June of that year to undertake supervisory duties over the maintenance of roads, footpaths and minor building works.[32] He also functioned as the collector of the town rates. In the same year, he was a candidate for the position of returning officer for the county council elections, receiving much support from south and east Galway based on his worthiness for the position and the ordeal of his prison sentence. At the November meeting of the county council, he was selected unanimously to supervise the elections held in the following year.[33]

The annual meeting of the south Galway UIL was held in Loughrea on 1 February 1914, and the main discussion points were the Land Bill and the Home Rule Bill that were currently before the House of Commons. In his speech, Finnegan said that the Land Bill afforded the prospect of a final settlement of the land question, but he regarded home rule as more important than all other issues. His political sympathies moved away from the UIL and the Irish Parliamentary Party, with strong public opposition to a recruitment drive for the Connaught Rangers in 1915 and an equally vehement rejection of conscription. He voiced support for the Easter Rising and regretted that ill health prevented him joining the Galway Volunteers at Moyode. The events of 1916 had an

28 For a detailed analysis of the dispute, see Campbell, *Land and revolution*, pp 153–65. 29 *Connaught Tribune*, 26 Aug. 1911. 30 *Connaught Tribune*, 5 June 1915. 31 *Connaught Tribune*, 2 Oct. 1915. 32 *Connaught Tribune*, 7 June 1913. 33 *Connaught Tribune*, 23 Nov. 1913.

impact on the south Galway UIL executive meeting in Loughrea on 1 October. The chairman, Willy Duffy, referred to the events of the Easter Rising and the 'fearless, unselfish, disinterested but, in my best judgment, mistaken and short-sighted men'.[34] The meeting pledged support for the constitutional approach of the UIL, but Finnegan voiced doubts about the current leadership of John Redmond and stated that the shelving of the Home Rule Bill was regrettable. He had nominated Willy Duffy for a number of parliamentary elections, but he did not support him for the general election of 1918 in which the Sinn Féin candidate, Frank Fahy, defeated Duffy.

The activities of the Loughrea TTA lapsed for a number of years and no meetings were held between September 1918 and March 1920. At the meeting held on 20 March 1920, Finnegan proposed that Lord Lascelles, who had inherited the Clanrickarde estate, should be approached to negotiate the sale of his interest in the Loughrea freehold and a deputation was nominated to meet Mr Morean, agent for the estate.[35] No progress was made with this iniative, and the TTA lapsed again until a public meeting was held to re-establish the branch in November 1922. Finnegan was elected chairman and, in his acceptance speech, he referred to a rumour that Lord Lascelles was willing to dispose of his interest in the town. He expressed the hope that 'the time was not too far distant when every tenant would become the rightful owner of his house'. A committee was nominated to commence negotiations with the estate.[36] Later that month, Mr Morean indicated that Lord Lascelles 'desired to approach the matter with the best wishes for the welfare of the town' and had opened discussions with his solicitor and Mr Coghlan Briscoe, general secretary of the national Town Tenants' League.[37] Negotiations continued over the following twelve months and the tenants made an offer of twelve years purchase in the gross rent. The TTA had undertaken to supply a list of those tenants willing to accept the proposal, but only twelve tenants had indicated that they were willing to pay on these terms.[38] In 1926, Finnegan resigned from the posts of town steward and town rate collector and was succeeded by his son, P.J. Finnegan. He was elected president of the TTA in May 1927, but there was no reference in the press report to negotiations with Lord Lascelles.[39] In September 1928, members of the town commissioners, TTA and Coghlan Briscoe held a meeting with the agent and solicitors for Lord Lascelles. In addition to the terms for purchase of the leasehold of the town, the purchase of the town hall, brewery and the tolls and customs were discussed. The meeting agreed to proceed with all of these matters and appointed a committee that included Finnegan and Duffy to conduct the negotiations. However, dissension developed between the town commissioners and the TTA and there was no report of any progress with negotiations on any of the issues.

34 *Connaught Tribune*, 7 Oct. 1916. 35 *Irish Times*, 20 Mar. 1920. 36 *Connaught Tribune*, 4 Nov. 1922. 37 *Connaught Tribune*, 9 Dec. 1922. 38 *Connaught Tribune*, 27 Dec. 1924. 39 *Connaught Tribune*, 21 May 1927.

Patrick Finnegan maintained a lively interest in national politics up to his death on 7 March 1939. At the funeral in Garrybreeda cemetery, the coffin was draped in the tricolour and carried by members of the Old IRA. The firing party was under the command of Commandant P.J. (Paddy) Kelly and Eamon Corbett, chairman of Galway County Council, delivered the funeral oration.[40] In the course of his speech, Corbett referred to Finnegan's leadership role in Craughwell during the Land War. He recalled the conviction of Finnegan and Muldowney by perjured evidence and a packed jury and their long period of imprisonment.

Patrick Finnegan's political allegiances
An obituary referred to Finnegan as the Fenian Centre for Craughwell, but it is known that John Newell was the Head Centre for the barony of Dunkellin at that time, and there is no documented evidence for this statement in police documents or the Fenian files in the National Archives. However, Finnegan made an interesting comment on the occasion of the erection of a memorial to the memory of Thomas Cunningham in Garrybreeda cemetery in October 1928. In a letter to the organizers, he referred to his imprisonment with Cunningham in Galway Jail at Christmas 1882. They had been arrested following the proclamation of the land meeting at Ballymana and, in the letter, Finnegan stated that he and Cunningham had been comrades in the Fenian organization at that time.

On the occasion of Finnegan's funeral, the oration referred to an invitation from Clan na Gael to visit America after his release from prison and that John Devoy was a personal friend. In addition, O'Donovan Rossa had welcomed him to America at a function in New York in 1904 and it is possible that Devoy was involved in the publication of the pamphlet, *The case of Patrick J. Finnegan*. When he attended the meeting of the Robert Emmet Literary Association in Butte on 13 July 1905, it was stated that he was a member of Camp 237 of Clan na Gael in Boston. This is the only documented evidence that he was a Fenian. The various functions organized to honour him were attended by the whole spectrum of Irish-American political interests, constitutional and revolutionary. There are no family recollections that he supported the campaign of agrarian violence during the Land War and following his trial and conviction he disclaimed any involvement in the killing of Peter Doherty or indeed of any connection with the boycotting of the family.

Finnegan's republican sympathies emerged in 1916 when on Easter Monday he expressed a desire to join the Galway Volunteers mobilized at Moyode Castle under Liam Mellows. However, illness occasioned by recurrent gout prevented him from doing so. The police may not have been aware of any possible association with the Volunteers because he was not included in the arrest and

40 *Connaught Tribune*, 18 Mar. 1939.

internment of Loughrea members immediately after the Easter Rising. In 1918, he voiced strong public opposition to conscription. During the War of Independence, he also expressed republican sympathies and was opposed to the signing of the treaty. He was an admirer of De Valera and, after its foundation, he supported Fianna Fáil and encouraged his son's active role as director of elections for south Galway. During the Blueshirt campaign, he berated a group of young men who had travelled from Craughwell to Loughrea for a meeting, telling them that they were a disgrace to their native village.

On balance, it would appear that the main thrust of his political activities after release from prison favoured a constitutional approach through the UIL and this view is supported by his willingness to seek a nomination for parliament in 1906 as a candidate for the Irish Parliamentary Party and subsequent support for Willy Duffy, the Irish Parliamentary Party MP. In later years, his allegiance moved to Sinn Féin and to Fianna Fáil, when it was founded in 1926. He lived to see the culmination of the important steps that had their origin in the period 1879–82 and which gradually led to the resolution of the land problem. These included the 1903 Land Act, successfully guided through parliament by George Wyndham, the chief secretary, who had signed the license for his release from jail. The amending Land Act of 1909 was the final effort by the British parliament and it improved facilities for land purchase and recognized the principle of compulsion. The foundation of the Irish Free State led to the implementation of measures to address the land problems, with particular relevance to Connacht. The Land Acts of 1923, 1931 and 1933 resulted in the strengthening of the powers of the Land Commission and, finally, after half a century, the realization of the famous slogans of the Land War: *The land for the people* and *Death to landlordism.*

Appendix 1

Persons from the Loughrea and Athenry police districts arrested under the Protection of Person and Property (Ireland) Act of 1881.[1]

Name	District	Arrested	Released	Suspected crime
M. Halloran	Loughrea	08 Mar. 1881	19 Apr. 1882	Preventing rent payment
T. Dolan	Loughrea	04 June 1881	17 Aug. 1882	Murder
P. Keogh	Loughrea	04 June 1881	17 Aug. 1882	Murder
E. Fahey	Loughrea	04 June 1881	17 Aug. 1882	Murder
J. Sweeney	Loughrea	10 June 1881	17 Aug. 1882	Accessory to murder
T. Cunningham	Loughrea	10 June 1881	17 Aug. 1882	Accessory to murder
J. Huban	Loughrea	10 June 1881	16 Apr. 1882	Accessory to murder
J. Ryan (1st)	Loughrea	17 June 1881	21 May 1882	Accessory to murder
J. Darcy	Loughrea	17 June 1881	17 Aug. 1882	Accessory to murder
M. Bermingham	Loughrea	17 June 1881	17 Aug. 1882	Accessory to murder
E. Barrett	Athenry	18 June 1881	23 Aug. 1882	Posting threatening notices
M. Connolly	Loughrea	09 July 1881	14 Mar. 1882	Treasonable practices
M. Glennon	Loughrea	09 July 1881	17 Aug. 1882	Posting threatening notices
M. Spellman	Loughrea	09 July 1881	01 Apr. 1882	Boycotting
M. Hooban	Loughrea	05 Nov. 1881	30 Apr. 1882	Intimidation against rent
J. Burke	Loughrea	05 Nov. 1881	29 June 1882	Intimidation against rent
P.C. Kelly	Athenry	09 Nov. 1881	23 Aug. 1882	Boycotting
P. Broderick	Athenry	09 Nov. 1881	23 Aug. 1882	Boycotting
J. Noakley	Loughrea	10 Nov. 1881	17 Aug. 1882	Firing into a dwelling
P. Tuohill	Loughrea	10 Nov. 1881	17 Aug. 1882	Firing into a dwelling
A. Keary	Loughrea	10 Nov. 1881	17 Aug. 1882	Boycotting
T.G. Griffin	Athenry	11 Nov. 1881	19 May 1882	Intimidation against rent
P. Morrissey	Athenry	25 Nov. 1881	23 Aug. 1882	Accessory to murder
T. Morrissey	Athenry	14 Nov. 1881	23 Aug. 1882	Accessory to murder
T. Coyne	Athenry	17 Nov. 1881	23 Aug. 1882	Intimidation against rent
T. Cunniffe	Athenry	25 Nov. 1881	23 Aug. 1882	Murder
J. Connors	Loughrea	24 Nov. 1881	19 May 1882	Intimidation against rent
P. Coughlan	Loughrea	24 Nov. 1881	08 Apr. 1882	Intimidation against rent

1 NAI Protection of Person and Propertry (Ireland) Act. List of all persons arrested, carton 1.

P. Plower	Loughrea	28 Nov. 1881	11 Apr. 1882	Intimidation against rent
M. Leahy	Loughrea	24 Nov. 1881	17 May 1882	Accessory to murder
A. Griffin	Athenry	03 Dec. 1881	12 Apr. 1882	Intimidation against rent
H. Pilkington	Loughrea	16 Dec. 1881	10 Apr. 1882	Intimidation against rent
J. Connaughton	Loughrea	16 Dec. 1881	18 May 1882	Intimidation against rent
J. Glennon	Loughrea	16 Dec. 1881	08 Apr. 1882	Intimidation against rent
P. Corbett	Athenry	29 Dec. 1881	21 May 1882	Intimidation against rent
J. Keane	Athenry	29 Dec. 1881	23 Aug. 1882	Intimidation against rent
D. Cunningham	Loughrea	29 Dec. 1881	12 Mar. 1882	Intimidation against rent
T. Duggan	Loughrea	29 Dec. 1881	26 May 1882	Intimidation against rent
M. Mullavel	Loughrea	29 Dec. 1881	20 Apr. 1882	Intimidation against rent
M. Calligy	Loughrea	29 Dec. 1881	16 Mar. 1882	Intimidation against rent
T. Cunningham	Loughrea	29 Dec. 1881	22 June 1882	Intimidation against rent
M. Furlong	Loughrea	29 Dec. 1881	25 Mar. 1882	Intimidation against rent
P. Kelly (1st)	Loughrea	29 Dec. 1881	03 May 1882	Intimidation against rent
T. Finnigan	Loughrea	27 Jan. 1882	06 June 1882	Intimidation against rent and boycotting
L. Quinn	Loughrea	27 Jan. 1882	11 Apr. 1882	Intimidation against rent
J. Kennedy	Loughrea	27 Jan. 1882	02 May 1882	Intimidation against rent
T. Keighrey	Loughrea	27 Jan. 1882	10 Apr. 1882	Intimidation against rent
J. McCarthy (1st)	Loughrea	27 Jan. 1882	08 June 1882	Intimidation against rent
J. Farrell (1st)	Loughrea	27 Jan. 1882	25 Feb. 1882	Intimidation against rent
N. Barrett	Loughrea	27 Jan. 1882	17 Aug. 1882	Intimidation against rent
M. Huban (1st)	Loughrea	27 Jan. 1882	17 Aug. 1882	Intimidation against rent
B. Coyle	Loughrea	27 Jan. 1882	17 Aug. 1882	Intimidation against rent
M. Dilleen (1st)	Loughrea	27 Jan. 1882	04 June 1882	Intimidation against rent

Peter Sweeney (1st)	Loughrea	27 Jan. 1882	11 Apr. 1882	Intimidation against rent
M. Greene (1st)	Loughrea	27 Jan. 1882	31 Mar. 1882	Intimidation against rent
H. Kennedy	Athenry	02 Feb. 1882	22 Aug. 1882	Intimidation against rent
P. Ruane	Athenry	27 Jan. 1882	07 June 1882	Intimidation against rent
J. Curley	Athenry	27 Jan. 1882	23 Aug. 1882	Intimidation against rent
M. Hynes	Athenry	27 Jan. 1882	23 Aug. 1882	Intimidation against rent
J. Moran	Athenry	27 Jan. 1882	23 Aug. 1882	Intimidation against rent
J. Melia	Athenry	27 Jan. 1882	15 Apr. 1882	Intimidation against rent
M. Kennedy	Athenry	02 Feb. 1882	09 June 1882	Intimidation against rent
M. Ward	Athenry	02 Feb. 1882	23 June 1882	Intimidation against rent
J. Broderick	Athenry	27 Jan. 1882	10 Apr. 1882	Intimidation against rent
J. Connelly	Athenry	02 Feb. 1882	08 June 1882	Intimidation against rent
P. Curley	Athenry	27 Jan. 1882	23 Aug. 1882	Intimidation against rent
P. Raftery	Loughrea	10 Feb. 1882	19 May 1882	Intimidation against rent
M. Minihan	Loughrea	10 Feb. 1882	21 May 1882	Intimidation against rent
P. Haverty	Loughrea	16 Feb. 1882	11 Apr. 1882	Intimidation against rent
James Buckley	Loughrea	10 Feb. 1882	08 Apr. 1882	Intimidation against rent
B. Stratford	Loughrea	10 Feb. 1882	17 May 1882	Intimidation against rent
M. Stratford	Loughrea	10 Feb. 1882	17 May 1882	Intimidation against rent
J. Coy	Loughrea	10 Feb. 1882	17 Aug. 1882	Intimidation against rent
J. Finnigan (1st)	Loughrea	10 Feb. 1882	31 Mar. 1882	Intimidation against rent
T. Halloran	Loughrea	10 Feb. 1882	07 June 1882	Intimidation against rent
John Buckley	Loughrea	10 Feb. 1882	09 Apr. 1882	Intimidation against rent
M. Cunningham	Loughrea	10 Feb. 1882	09 Apr. 1882	Intimidation against rent

T. Haire (1st)	Loughrea	10 Feb. 1882	21 May 1882	Inciting to murder
J. Coane	Athenry	28 Feb. 1882	23 Aug. 1882	Shooting at person
T. Coane	Athenry	28 Feb. 1882	23 Aug. 1882	Shooting at person
J. McGann	Athenry	28 Feb. 1882	23 Aug. 1882	Shooting at person
P. Gilligan	Athenry	28 Feb. 1882	11 Apr. 1882	Shooting at person
P. Finnegan	Athenry	17 Apr. 1882	23 Aug. 1882	Murder
J. McCarthy (2nd)	Loughrea	04 July 1882	17 Aug. 1882	Accessory to murder
Peter Sweeney (2nd)	Loughrea	04 July 1882	17 Aug. 1882	Accessory to murder
M. Kennedy	Loughrea	04 July 1882	17 Aug. 1882	Accessory to murder
W. Manahan	Loughrea	04 July 1882	17 Aug. 1882	Accessory to murder
P. Burke	Loughrea	04 July 1882	17 Aug. 1882	Accessory to murder
P. Morrissey	Loughrea	04 July 1882	17 Aug. 1882	Accessory to murder
J. Ryan (2nd)	Loughrea	04 July 1882	17 Aug. 1882	Accessory to murder
M. Dilleen (2nd)	Loughrea	04 July 1882	17 Aug. 1882	Accessory to murder
M. Butler	Loughrea	04 July 1882	17 Aug. 1882	Accessory to murder
J. Finnigan (2nd)	Loughrea	04 July 1882	17 Aug. 1882	Accessory to murder
M. Huban (2nd)	Loughrea	04 July 1882	17 Aug. 1882	Accessory to murder
J. McDermot	Loughrea	04 July 1882	17 Aug. 1882	Accessory to murder
A. McEntee	Loughrea	04 July 1882	17 Aug. 1882	Accessory to murder
Patrick Sweeney	Loughrea	04 July 1882	17 Aug. 1882	Accessory to murder
M. Clarke	Loughrea	04 July 1882	17 Aug. 1882	Accessory to murder
M. Greene (2nd)	Loughrea	04 July 1882	17 Aug. 1882	Accessory to murder
P. Corry	Loughrea	04 July 1882	17 Aug. 1882	Accessory to murder
T. O'Brien	Loughrea	04 July 1882	17 Aug. 1882	Accessory to murder
F. O'Neill	Loughrea	04 July 1882	17 Aug. 1882	Accessory to murder
P. Kavanagh	Loughrea	04 July 1882	17 Aug. 1882	Accessory to murder
W. Flynn	Loughrea	04 July 1882	17 Aug. 1882	Accessory to murder
J. Farrell (2nd)	Loughrea	04 July 1882	17 Aug. 1882	Accessory to murder
W. Delaney	Loughrea	04 July 1882	17 Aug. 1882	Accessory to murder
M. Leahy	Loughrea	07 July 1882	17 Aug. 1882	Accessory to murder
T. Connolly	Loughrea	17 July 1882	17 Aug. 1882	Accessory to murder
J. Connaire	Loughrea	17 July 1882	17 Aug. 1882	Accessory to murder
P. Kelly (2nd)	Loughrea	18 July 1882	17 Aug. 1882	Inciting to murder
E. Costello	Loughrea	18 July 1882	17 Aug. 1882	Inciting to murder
T. Haire (2nd)	Loughrea	18 July 1882	17 Aug. 1882	Inciting to murder
J. Sheill	Loughrea	18 July 1882	17 Aug. 1882	Accessory to murder
M. Fogarty	Loughrea	18 July 1882	17 Aug. 1882	Accessory to murder
T Pendergast	Loughrea	18 July 1882	17 Aug. 1882	Accessory to murder
T. Joyce	Loughrea	18 July 1882	17 Aug. 1882	Accessory to murder
P. Connelly	Loughrea	19 July 1882	17 Aug. 1882	Accessory to murder
M. Cusack	Loughrea	21 July 1882	17 Aug. 1882	Accessory to murder
M. Connolly	Loughrea	19 July 1882	17 Aug. 1882	Accessory to murder
M. Connolly	Loughrea	21 July 1882	17 Aug. 1882	Accessory to murder

Appendix 2

Persons arrested after the Irish National League meeting in Ballymana in December 1882.[2]

Thomas Cunningham	Loughrea
E.J. Barrett	Craughwell
N.J. Barrett	Loughrea
James McDermott	Loughrea
Michael Connelly	Ballymana
John Joyce	
Peter Joyce	Grenage
Martin Kelly	Roo
Tom. Kelly	Roo
Thomas Holland	
Thomas Cunniffe	Cahergal
Michael Cloonan	Caherfurvaus
Peter Skehill	Craughwell
Pat. Kineen	Craughwell
Thomas Carr	Killora
John Connean	
Patrick Finnegan	Aggard
Michael Fogarty	Shanbally
John Kennedy	Ballylin E.
Michael [Martin?] Roland	
John Glynn	Craughwell
John Newell	Carrigans
John Ryan	Mannin
Thomas Stratford	
James Coy	
Pat Connelly	Lisnagrieve
Thomas Finnegan	Kilconieran
Patrick Raftery	
Michael Connolly	Ballywinna
M. Kennedy	
Martin Whelan	
John Duane	Rathruddy
Martin Mannion	

Thomas Stratford, James Coy and John Duane were released on bail pending their appeal. The appeal was upheld by Judge T. Rice Henn Esq., QC.[3]

2 *Western News*, 30 Dec. 1882; 7 Jan. 1883.   3 *Galway Vindicator*, 27 Jan. 1883.

Bibliography

MANUSCRIPT SOURCES

British Library
Spencer papers

Butte-Silver Bow Public Archives
Robert Emmet Literary Association Minute Book
Ancient Order of Hibernians Minute Book

James Hardiman Library, NUIG
PRO, CO 904
Special Collections

Military Archives, Bureau of Military History, WS 1,562

National Archives of Ireland, Dublin
Chief Secretary's Office, Registered Papers
Crime Branch Special
Criminal Record File
Irish Land League and Irish National League documents
Protection of Person and Property (Ireland) Act of 1881

National Library of Ireland
Parnell Special Commission (London, 1890)

Private possessions
Letter of John (Soldier) Morrissey in possession of Maura Lyons
Letter of Peter Sweeney in possession of the present author
Letter of Michael Clasby in possession of Gerry Cloonan

Parliamentary papers
HC 1884 (80), lxiii, 529. Return of awards by lord lieutenant of Ireland under Crimes
    Act, and by Grand Juries in Ireland under Peace Preservation (Ireland) Act of 1875.

Acts
Encumbered Estates (Ireland) Act, 12 & 13 Vict., c. 77, 1849.
Protection of Person and Property (Ireland) Act, 44 & 45 Vict., c. 14, 1881.
Prevention of Crime (Ireland) Act, 45 & 46 Vict., c. 25, 1882.

Newspapers
Boston Pilot
Connaught People

Connaught Tribune
Freeman's Journal
Gaelic American
Galway Express
Galway Free Press
Galway Observer
Galway Vindicator
Illustrated London News
Independent and Nation
Irish World and American Industrial Liberator
Leitrim Advertiser
Pall Mall Gazette
Sligo Champion
The Blazer
The Graphic
The Irish Times
The Leader
Tuam Herald
Tuam News
Western News

UNPUBLISHED SOURCES

Ball, Stephen Andrew, 'Policing the Land War: official responses to political protest
    and agrarian crime in Ireland, 1879–91' (PhD, U London, 2000).
Lyons, Maura, unpublished history of Rahasane House.

PUBLISHED SOURCES

Berry, James, *My experiences as an executioner*, ed. H. Snowden Ward (London, 1892).
Campbell, Fergus, *Land and revolution* (Oxford, 2005).
Carey, Tim, *Mountjoy: the story of a prison* (Cork, 2000).
Cawley, Thomas, *An Irish parish: its sunshine and shadows* (Boston, 1911).
Clancy, John J., *Six months of 'Unionist' rule* (London, 1887).
Joe Clarke, 'It's not fit for you to be keeping company with that unfortunate fellow' in
    Sweeney (ed.), *Hanging crimes* (2005).
Coogan, Tim Pat, *The man who made Ireland* (London, 1990).
Corfe, Tom, *The Phoenix Park murders: conflict, compromise and tragedy in Ireland,
    1879–1882* (London, 1968).
Counsel, E.P.S., *Jury packing* (Dublin, 1887).
Crilly, Daniel, *Jury packing in Ireland* (Dublin, 1887).
Emmons, David M., *The Butte Irish, class and ethnicity in an American mining town,
    1875–1925* (Urbana & Chicago, 1989).

Finnegan, Patrick J., *The case of Patrick J. Finnegan: an Irish patriot, victim of the English government* (New York, 1904).

Foy, Michael T., *Michael Collins's intelligence war* (Stroud, 2006).

Gordon, Peter, *The Red Earl* (Northampton, 1981).

Hart, Peter, *Mick* (London, 2005).

Johnson, D.S., 'Trial by jury in Ireland, 1860–1914', *Journal of Legal History*, 17:3 (Dec. 1996), 270–93.

Jordan, Kieran (ed.), *Kiltullagh/Killimordaly as the centuries passed: a history from 1500–1900* (Kiltullagh/Killimordaly, 2000).

Kelly Desmond, Catherine, 'John Henry Blake: villain or victim?' in Jordan (ed.), *Kiltullagh/Killimordaly as the centuries passed: a history from 1500–1900* (2000).

Lane, Padraig G., 'The general impact of the Encumbered Estates Act of 1849 on Counties Galway and Mayo', *Journal of Galway Archaelogical and Historical Society*, 33 (1972–3), 44–74.

Lane, Padraig G., 'The Encumbered Estates Court and Galway land ownership, 1849–58' in Gerard Moran & Raymond Gillespie (eds), *Galway: history and society* (Dublin, 1996).

Lourdes Fahy, Sr Mary de, *Kiltartan: many leaves, one root* (Kiltartan, 2004).

Matthew, H.C.G., & Brian Harrison (eds), *Oxford dictionary of national biography* (Oxford, 2004).

McConville, Sean, *Irish political prisoners* (London, 2003).

McEldowney, John F., 'Some aspects of law and policy in the administration of criminal justice in nineteenth-century Ireland' in J.F. McEldowney & P. O'Higgins, *The common law tradition: essays in Irish legal history* (Dublin, 1990).

McGee, Owen, *The IRB* (Dublin, 2005).

Milroy, Sean, *Memories of Mountjoy* (London, Dublin, 1917).

Mitchel, John, *Jail journal* (Dublin, 1914).

Moody, T.W., & R.A.J. Hawkins (eds), *Florence Arnold-Forster's Irish journal* (Oxford, 1988).

Moran, Gerard, & Raymond Gillespie (eds), *Galway: history and society* (Dublin, 1996).

O'Brien, William, & Desmond Ryan (eds), *Devoy's post bag* (Dublin, 1948).

Ryan David, 'The trial and execution of Anthony Daly', *Loughrea history project* (Loughrea, 2003), i, p. 99.

Sweeney, Frank (ed.), *Hanging crimes* (Cork 2005).

Thom's Directory.

Tynan, P.J.P., *The Irish National Invincibles and their times* (London, 1894).

Vaughan, W.E., *Murder trials in Ireland, 1836–1914* (Dublin, 2009).

Waldron, Jarlath, *Maamtrasna: the murders and the mystery* (Dublin 1992).

Wemyss Reid, Thomas, *Life of the Rt Hon. W.E. Forster* (New York, 1970).

Index